REFUEL

>> AN UNCOMPLICATED GUIDE TO CONNECTING WITH GOD //

Also by **Doug Fields**

Among others . . .

Congratulations . . . You're Gifted!
Creative Bible Lessons on the Life of Christ
Help! I'm a Student Leader
One Minute Bible
Purpose Driven Youth Ministry
Speaking to Teenagers
What Matters Most

For a comprehensive list of the 50+ books
Doug has authored and coauthored, please visit
www.dougfields.com.

REFUEL

>> AN UNCOMPLICATED GUIDE TO CONNECTING WITH GOD //

DOUG FIELDS

THOMAS NELSON
Since 1798

NASHVILLE   DALLAS   MEXICO CITY   RIO DE JANEIRO   BEIJING

Published in Nashville, Tennessee, by Thomas Nelson. Thomas Nelson is a
registered trademark of Thomas Nelson, Inc.

Thomas Nelson, Inc., titles may be purchased in bulk for educational, business,
fund-raising, or sales promotional use. For information, please e-mail
SpecialMarkets@ThomasNelson.com.

Unless otherwise noted, Scripture quotations are taken from the *Holy Bible*, New
Living Translation, copyright © 1996. Used by permission of Tyndale House
Publishers, Inc., Wheaton, Illinois 60189. All rights reserved.

Scripture quotations marked MSG are from *The Message* by Eugene H. Peterson. ©
1993, 1994, 1995, 1996, 2000. Used by permission of NavPress Publishing Group.
All rights reserved.

Scripture quotations marked NIV are from the HOLY BIBLE: NEW INTERNATIONAL
VERSION®. Copyright © 1973, 1978, 1984 by International Bible Society. Used by
permission of Zondervan. All rights reserved.

Library of Congress Cataloging-in-Publication Data

Fields, Doug, 1962–
  Refuel : an uncomplicated way to connect with God / Doug Fields.
      p. cm.
  Includes bibliographical references and index.
  ISBN 978-0-8499-2054-7
  1. Spiritual life—Christianity. I. Title.
BV4501.3.F54 2008
248.4—dc22   2008013239

Printed in the United States of America

14 15 16 17 QG 7 6 5 4

//

Dedication

would like to dedicate this book to the people who call Saddleback Church their home. I love being one of your pastors! I love teaching you the Bible. I love your passion for learning. I love your concern for your neighbors. I love your commitment to pursuing God in all areas of your lives. I love your dedication to giving—and giving generously. I love talking to you and hearing about what God is doing in your lives. I love you! I'm living the dream of pastoring people (young and old) who want to connect with God. Thank you for being church to me and my family. I can't imagine serving anywhere else.

Acknowledgments

have never really done anything worthwhile without tapping into the help and community of others— this book is no exception. I am deeply grateful for several friends who played instrumental roles in reading the manuscript and offering me suggestions that made this a more helpful book. Thank you, Brian Bird, Marcus Brotherton, Marla Christian, Lisa and Steve Gladen, Angela Griffin, Craig Hodgkins, Mike Howerton, Tom Holladay, Buddy Owens, Jana Sarti, Ross Schaffer, Rob and MaryLynn Vollmer, and Linda Vujnov. I'm also indebted to my agent, Greg Johnson, for believing that I have something to offer. Heartfelt thanks to my pastor, friend, and mentor, Rick Warren, for believing in me and allowing me the privilege of teaching at Saddleback Church (where this material first developed). I always acknowledge my kids because they are the loves of my life and have taught me more about God than anyone. My prayer is that you—Torie, Cody, and Cassie—will grow up to live out the principles in this book. I love watching your faith grow—you all inspire me. Finally, the depths of my thanks go to my wife, Cathy, who models what I've written and maintains a connection with God and a confidence for living that I haven't seen in anyone else. I'm so grateful for you, and I'm blessed to journey with you!

Contents

I'm a Spiritual Loser

Within one week of getting his driver's license, my sixteen-year-old son came to me feeling discouraged. He'd been thrilled to pass his driving test, but now his body language was unusually lifeless as he approached me. He said, "Dad, I need to talk to you about my car." Immediately I thought he was going to tell me about a speeding ticket or a fender bender or something that would cause him pain and cost me money. Instead, I discovered that his flat persona resulted from his need for additional cash to refuel his car. His weekly gas budget only lasted two and a half days, and now his tank—and his wallet—were empty. He was shocked at how few miles he could travel on one tank of gas.

Sadly he said, "Dad, I gauged it all wrong. I had no idea I'd go empty so soon."

His older sister had "blessed" him with the family hand-me-down car (which she got from her great-grandmother) before she went off to college. Now, sixteen-year-old Cody Fields, varsity athlete, at the height of impressing every living creature under the age of eighteen, was the one driving the 1990 Buick LaSabre. If you don't know this model, just think "tank." To suggest it isn't fuel efficient would be an understatement. Then add the color maroon to it, throw on a few stickers (such as "I [heart] Kenya"), several little dents, and two missing hubcaps. While Cody doesn't adore the car, he's wise enough not to complain, because it would trigger Dad Lecture #317: "Gratefulness."

When he was learning to drive, he'd jump in and out of the family car without ever considering the implications of a low fuel level. To his inexperienced mind, cars always seemed to have enough. He had been taught the basics of pumping gas but never really connected the price of gas to his own wallet and what happens when you unexpectedly and all too quickly reach empty. He was definitely not the first young driver to admit, "I had no idea I'd go empty so soon."

Cody's experience was very similar to how many Christians feel: living on empty, in need of spiritual refueling, and not exactly sure what to do. But unlike an empty automobile tank, followers of Jesus can be spiritually empty yet appear as though nothing is wrong—and some are great actors. For example, I can *pretend* all is well without confessing my emptiness or bringing others into my need for refueling. It's very easy to live *as* if my spiritual tank is full. I can just put my life in cruise mode. I'll be the first to admit that it's not spiritually healthy, but I can do it easily. So can you. Unfortunately, *cruise mode* is common practice for too many Christ-followers, and I want that to change. I'm hoping you do too.

> **Followers of Jesus can be spiritually empty yet appear as though nothing is wrong—and some are great actors.**

Over the course of my own spiritual journey, I've become very aware that if I don't connect with God on a regular basis, I run out of passion and become spiritually empty. Just like the gas in my son's car, my spiritual life drains more quickly (and more frequently) than I anticipate. And it's not a pretty sight.

When I'm spiritually empty, my life sputters. Things feel different. Not good different—bad different. I'm shallow, confused, and anxious. Again, I can pretend to be full and fool others, but my emptiness is embarrassingly apparent to me. When my needle is nearing the red, there are some obvious warning signs:

» I'm more selfish with my time.
» I'm impatient.
» I lack compassion for those who are hurting.
» I'm more vulnerable to temptation.
» I begin to act like I deserve certain things.
» I'm short with people.
» I'm disobedient.
» I feel distant from God.
» I'm cynical.
» I find it more difficult to make good decisions.
» My insecurities are more prevalent.
» I begin to look to others to fill voids that I know only God can fill.
» I'm critical—in speech as well as thought.

And that's only a partial list (after all, this is a short book). I realize those symptoms aren't attractive. And I'm aware that this isn't what Jesus meant when He called me to be the "light of the world" (Matthew 5:14). I would even understand if you closed the book and thought, *Yikes! This guy is a follower of Christ, and he acts like that?* But I'm betting you won't stop reading, because my guess is that if you're really honest, your list probably looks similar to mine. Am I right?

How do you act when you're spiritually empty? Have you ever spent time reflecting on how being disconnected from God impacts you? If not, it's a great exercise, and I encourage you to do it so you can become aware of what happens when you're nearing empty.

Become aware of what happens when you're nearing empty.

For example, you might have abnormal anger in your life and not be aware that it's connected to your spiritual emptiness. You uncharacteristically snap at your kids, you're less patient with your coworkers, or you lean too heavily on the horn while driving. All of a sudden, everyone on the road is an idiot, and you're the poster child for the National Association of Good Drivers. Yeah, right! You know what's happening? You're living on E.

Perhaps your emptiness translates into a passion for food. Evening comes and you ransack the cupboards looking for salty or sugary treats. Then, halfway through a gallon of ice cream, you realize you're not eating out of physical hunger—you're eating because you're bored, tired, annoyed, hurting, stressed, anxious, worried, or desperate. Again, you're spiritually empty.

Or maybe you're the type who goes shopping when your spiritual tank is in the red. The money's not in your wallet, but credit cards are—four of them! Three hours, six stores, and two hundred dollars later, you're on a spending high, but inside you're as barren as when you started. Empty.

Though your symptoms may be different from those of others, spiritual emptiness is universal—yes, even for the people filling up our churches. So many of my Christian friends have confessed that when they aren't filled up spiritually, the pressures of life begin to squeeze into their souls and occupy space that God once filled. They are overflowing with these pressures rather than with the presence of God. Can you relate to this feeling at all?

I had experienced emptiness so many times that I finally decided to take some radical actions. I went public. I admitted it. First, I confessed my emptiness to close friends. And much to my surprise, they didn't reject me; instead, they passionately identified. I was blown away! I had always thought I was alone in my recurring emptiness. But once I found the courage to talk about it, I realized I was *not* alone. Then, not only did I converse about it, I began to *preach* on it. When I was truthful about my own spiritual emptiness, I found people in my church really wanting to talk about theirs. And now I'm putting it in a book, knowing that the masses will relate (at least the honest ones).

While I believe this book will be very helpful for new believers, I'm really writing to *anyone* who wants more out of their relationship with God. New or old. Is that you? Do you want to be spiritually different? Do you want to be filled with more of God and less of yourself? If so, it would bring me great joy to help you connect with God on a regular basis in a way that is uncomplicated and guilt free. Your life will be so much richer when you're spiritually full. And there is hope ahead, my friend! You can learn to consistently refuel your spiritual tank and experience the fullness of life that God promises. You don't need to run on empty anymore.

The Reality of Unrealistic Expectations

If you've spent any amount of time in church, it's safe to assume you've heard a sermon or two (or a hundred) about the need to connect with God on a regular basis. We pastor-types often refer to this action as "quiet time" or "devotions" or "vespers." We usually preach on some basic formulas that include daily Bible reading and prayer. Our sermons are then supplemented with similar messages in Christian books and magazine articles that also encourage Christ-followers to develop and maintain spiritual disciplines.

Countless Christians listen to these sermons and then try out these formulas to develop spiritual habits that will keep them filled. They purchase study guides, daily devotionals, and read-through-the-Bible-in-a-year Bibles. They confidently set their alarm clocks to wake up earlier in the morning; prop open their Bibles, then their eyes; and joyfully attempt to study God's Word, all the while, thinking, *I'm going to read this dang Bible if it kills me.* Sounds familiar, doesn't it? But here's what it *really* looks like:

Day 1: You do it. You check off that you read and prayed. Way to go!

Day 2: You do it again. Well done! Connecting with God is easy, right?

Day 3: You have a "quiet time" for a third day in a row. You're awesome! Well, kind of, but since you read so fast, you don't really remember anything an hour later.

Day 4: You want to do it, but you're so tired that you tell yourself you'll do it later in the day . . . but you don't. It was a long day, and now your favorite show is on TV.

Day 5: It's a Sunday, so you gave yourself a "bye day," because church is basically an extended quiet time where you're getting spiritually filled. You'll get back on track with your new disciplines tomorrow morning. (Plus, Monday is the same day you always start your new diet.)

Day 6: Monday. Too tired after a long weekend. Need the extra sleep. Hit snooze button. Feel a little guilty, but the tiredness drowns out the guilt.

Day 7 and following: During the next week or so, you find some victory with your program, but you meet more defeat. Guilt reemerges because you're not as consistent as you want to be. Even when you do connect with God, you're tired and unfocused. It feels forced, more like obligation than desire. You're just going through the motions in order to check off that box that will haunt you if it's empty.

Soon you quit that early morning "habit" (not sure it was long-lived enough to officially be titled a habit). You don't quit out of disgust. You don't quit out of frustration. You just quietly stop.

If that describes you, please know that you're not alone. Actually, you're most likely in the majority. Your problem isn't the lack of desire. You truly crave a connection with God. You want your heart to be full. You long to know God more deeply and be more intimately connected to Him. So what's wrong? Why does connecting with God seem so difficult to do?

The problem appears when unrealistic expectations are attached to an unrealistic plan.

I believe the problem appears when unrealistic expectations are attached to an unrealistic plan. You agreed to an unreasonable plan. You couldn't figure out how to weave it into the life you already lead. The good habit you tried to form proved unsustainable. It just didn't work for you. Again, you're not alone. According to research, only about half of all Christian adults have a regular "quiet time"—and even then, they connect with God on their own only about one time a week.[1]

And based on my experiences and conversations as a pastor for more than twenty-five years, I'd bet even fewer are connecting with God on a regular basis than those numbers indicate.

As I already mentioned, I know that failure and the disappointment it brings all too well. I have a strong desire to know God and His Word—really, I do. And I, too, have tried the "through the Bible in a year" plan for . . . uh, I don't know . . . twenty years? I hate to admit it, but I always fail. Always! I've read Genesis more times than anyone on the planet. I start off with a bang in January, but because I need to read three chapters every single day to stay on track, by mid-February I'm so far behind that I've got to try to read all of Leviticus in one sitting to catch up (it's next to impossible—at least if I plan to understand what I'm reading). It's like that diet I start every Monday, when my best intentions get thrown at those ten extra pounds, but nothing ever seems to

---

1. The Barna Group, "The State of the Church 2000," Barna Update, www.barna.org.

change. Even though I genuinely *want* to connect with God, I can't keep up with that strategy. And because I don't, I feel guilty. *I must not be a very good Christian,* I think miserably.

Guilt and Comparison

Most Christians claim to want to connect with God regularly—or at least they want the benefits of the richer spiritual life that result from consistent connections. But when it comes to turning desire into discipline, most don't. Failure gives birth to guilt.

This guilt can be crushing. Wonderful men and women (like you) limp through the Christian life marred by it. It's guilt, guilt, guilt 24/7—*I don't pray enough. I'm not reading the Bible like I should. I haven't witnessed to my neighbor. I don't spend enough time with God . . .* Guilty.

If guilt defines you, I'm so sorry. I pray that you'll come to see that you're not a "lousy Christian" if you don't have a traditional quiet time. The Christian life is not about locks and chains. Jesus Christ came to set us free. Yes, some guilt may serve as God's motivator, but too many Christians cower because of false guilt—aka *condemnation*—that they've heaped upon their own shoulders because they've compared themselves to an unrealistic model and come up short. That type of guilt is wrong and unfair, and it will weigh you down and wear you out.

Comparison is deadly, yet so natural. It's easy to place ourselves next to someone we *think* has it together spiritually, constantly taking mental notes on how we don't measure up. Yet comparison only *assumes* that others are doing what we're not, and so we end up contrasting what we know about ourselves (everything) with what we don't really know about others (which is almost everything). Again, not fair.

Then, to make matters worse, we hear stories about people such as Martin Luther, who awoke each day at 4:00 a.m. and spent hours with God. "I have so much to do today that I should spend the first three hours in prayer," he said. Now, that *really* piles on the guilt. I'm really happy for Martin Luther that he was able to pull that off. But, as for me, I'm *not* a morning person. I didn't even know there was a 4:00 a.m. until I read his quote in seminary.

How about Mother Teresa's famous saying: "Spend one hour a day in adoration of your Lord and never do anything you know is wrong, and you will be all right." Yeah, right! I'd much rather hear something about how she couldn't find her Bible because she hadn't read it in two weeks. I'd love a quote like that! "Amen!" I'd say. "Preach it, sister. Share another failure so I don't feel like a spiritual loser!" Oh well, I guess just the great ones make it into the quote books that supply pastors' sermons.

My dear brothers and sisters in Christ—please read this very carefully—there's a good reason why Mother Teresa and Martin Luther were recognized for their faith: one spent forty years in Calcutta and won the Nobel Peace Prize for working with the world's poorest of the poor; the other turned all of Christendom on its head. Their greatness wasn't just in their accomplishments; they were also deeply dependent and consistent in their relationship with God. And if you're *anything* like me, well, then you're almost *nothing* like them. Most days we feel more like Mother Goose than Mother Teresa. That's because, in comparison, you and I are ordinary people who live ordinary lives: we're carpool parents juggling jam-packed schedules; businesspeople balancing careers and family; university students carrying full class loads; new moms and dads figuring out how to get children to sleep so we can find a few minutes of quiet; grandparents who are active in families and communities.

Please stop comparing. You're not Mother Teresa

or Martin Luther. Neither am I. You're you! God designed you to be you in your faith too. I'm not suggesting that you can't have an intimacy with God similar to that of other heroes of our faith; of course you can. But I'm asking you to quit comparing, and instead be challenged to learn how to be spiritually refueled in realistic ways that fit with how you're wired. You can do this! I know you can.

Learn how to be spiritually refueled in realistic ways that fit how you're wired.

I'm so excited that you care enough about your spiritual life to take time to read and learn and increase your intimacy with God. My prayer is that this little book becomes a source of refreshment for you. But before you turn to the next chapter, take a minute—right now—and ask God to relieve you of the trap of comparison and guilt and to help you embrace that relief. Then, come on! Let's continue the journey.

This Week: Consider the ways in which you compare yourself to others in your daily life. When you catch yourself doing it, focus on the truth that God created you to be unique, and that He doesn't compare you to anyone.

Reflect: What do you think God might be saying to you after reading this chapter?

How have you felt like a spiritual loser when you compare yourself to others? Who is someone who could help you stay refueled and feel like a spiritual winner?

Prayer: Lord, thank You for creating me with all of my gifts, faults, and failings, and for loving me anyway. Thank You that You never compare me to anyone else, and that You see me through the perfect eyes of Your son, Jesus.

Ditch the Guilt

When I was a small child, I remember hearing someone refer to God as a vacuum cleaner. I know it sounds odd, but I have a distinct memory of hearing the words "God-shaped vacuum" and taking them literally. I didn't understand that the person was actually talking about a God-shaped *void* rather than the item in our downstairs closet. Whoever used those words didn't really appreciate the limitations of my vocabulary, or he would have chosen a better word—like *emptiness*.

Anyway, I grew up thinking God looked like a Hoover. I'm sure it struck me as odd at the time that God would be shaped like a vacuum cleaner, but I was young and didn't know enough about God to argue. So when my family would say a prayer at Christmas or Easter, I imagined a celestial vacuum cleaner being the recipient of our words.

During this age of confusion, my mom made a generous offer to make me any type of Halloween costume I wanted. I could only think of one thing—I wanted to dress up like God. She said, "Doug, I don't know what God looks like." I scoffed at my mother's theological ignorance and pulled the red Hoover upright out of the closet. "He looks like this, but bigger. If I'm a vacuum cleaner, I can suck up everyone's candy." My immature comment was followed by Mom's laughter, a corrective lecture on the nature of God, and the promise to make me a bumblebee costume.

Now, I'd rather you think of me as cute than as dumb, but I would understand if you chose the latter. I have told this story many times, and if my mom happens to be nearby at the time, she'll proudly add, "And he looked so cute as a bee." But often, after telling the story, I ask my audience (if they stick around), "How do you view God?" This specific question is usually followed by a pause, an uncomfortable look of consideration, and then an answer that seems to be very common: *Someone who is disappointed—even angry—at me.* Many of my friends would respond the same way. It's sad, but that description makes sense when you consider how many people feel guilty because they're trying to please an angry God.

What about you? How do you view God? I hope your view of Him doesn't elicit guilt.

Jesus despised those who piled on the guilt. Nothing seemed to anger Him as quickly as the unrealistic expectations of religious leaders. In fact, He had strong words for those who established and enforced guilt-inducing rules and regulations. He even called them some very unflattering names: Vipers. Snakes. Hypocrites. Blind guides. Whitewashed tombs. Yikes! Imagining Jesus using those words evokes an image very different from the smiling Jesus carrying a baby sheep on His shoulders. But that's exactly what He called the Pharisees and teachers of the law who made it so hard for people to come to God. And that's not all that made Him mad. In addition to their guilt-producing expectations, these religious types also loved to *show* how religious they were—just so people would see and applaud them. On their heads and forearms they wore big, fat *phylacteries* (yeah, I don't know how to pronounce it either), conspicuous leather pouches containing strips of parchments bearing Old Testament verses. They sought out places of honor and loved being called "rabbi," a title that implied that they were important scholars. Even the tassels of their prayer shawls were long and noticeable enough for everyone to see and admire. But Jesus said to watch out for these leaders.

Jesus despised those who piled on the guilt.

"They tie up heavy loads and put them on men's shoulders, but they themselves are not willing to lift a finger to move them. Everything they do is done for men to see" (Matthew 23:4–5a NIV). *They crush others with impossible religious demands.*

My prayer for the impact of this book is just the opposite. I don't want to crush you with impossible religious demands. I want you to discover and experience spiritual liberty. I want to cut the straps of the heavy guilt loads you carry and watch them roll down the street, out of your sight and memory forever. I want you to stop feeling guilty. I want to invite you to escape the burdensome ways you may have become accustomed to and make connections with God that bring rest for your soul. That's what Jesus wants too (Matthew 11:28–30).

A Compartmentalized Faith

To minimize the guilt and maximize your connections with God, I'm convinced that you have to fight against living out a *compartmentalized faith*. What is that? A compartmentalized faith is a pick-and-choose lifestyle in which a person basically wanders between a Christlike life and a Christless life. Typically such a person chooses to live God's way when the church lights are on and Christian friends are looking, but behind closed doors, when no eye can see him, all bets are off.

Speaking of bets, a compartmentalized faith fits very well with the famous Las Vegas ad campaign: "What happens in Vegas, stays in Vegas." Think about what that implies. Hey, you want to cheat on your spouse in Vegas? No problem, it all stays there. Want to gamble away all your savings? Vegas will never tell. Want to party till you puke? Fine. The smell will never make it to your home. The implication of this approach is that it's okay, even desirable, to live one way in Vegas, then another way at home. A compartmentalized faith is basically the same thing: "What happens away from church, stays away from church." It's a weak, shallow, and empty faith, and it attracts guilt.

Here's what it might look like in the real world: You go to a weekly church service and feel inspired. You get spiritually filled—it's great. You and God are tight. On the way out of church, you feel so good that you want to pass out flowers and hug strangers. You get in your car feeling happy, and you politely encourage other cars to pull ahead. ("Oh, you go first, brother; there's a lot of love in this car right now.") You even consider picking up a hitchhiker on the way home, but since he's wearing a hockey mask, you smile and wave instead. You go home, wash the dishes with a peppy whistle, cut your neighbor's lawn because he's gone on vacation, smile as you grocery shop, and actually return the shopping cart to the little cart corral—all while still feeling filled up from the time at church.

Then Monday arrives. You get to work and learn that your boss wants a major project completed two weeks ahead of time. No one brewed coffee in the break room, and that nut ball in the cubicle next to yours has stolen your favorite pen again. All the faith-filled feelings from yesterday fly right into the toilet. It's game on! Survival! What happens away from church, stays away from church. The evil thoughts that bubble up in your heart are real, and you want to obey those feelings. *Jesus who?*

Here's my personal experience: when I'm spiritually empty, I naturally gravitate toward a compartmentalized faith. I hate to admit it, but when I'm not feeling close to God, the actions of the world are attractive and even seductive to me. Worse, not only do I lean toward compartmentalization, but I also end up feeling guilty for every decision that wasn't God-honoring. Thankfully, as I've grown in my faith, I've also learned to recognize the signs of my spiritual emptiness. Now I can usually catch myself *before* I experience the negative consequences of my actions.

I remember one time when it was very obvious to me that I was approaching spiritual "E." I felt distant from God. It was an overly busy time in my life—I was rushing around from meeting to meeting, and I wasn't connecting with God. And on this one particular day, instead of practicing what I preach and taking time to stop, be quiet, and make a connection with God, I chose to stop at a loud restaurant and connect with food. I was in a hurry to get to an appointment but had just enough time to go to In-N-Out Burger for my favorite "Double-Double, Animal-Style." Timewise I was cutting it a little tight, but if everything went according to plan, I would be okay. Unfortunately, it didn't go according to plan.

The problem was with the young lady taking orders—she didn't share my sense of urgency. She was focused on trading lip-gloss tips with her friend instead of expediting the line.

I tried to drop hints. I tapped my fingers. I made broad, glancing gestures at my watch. But she went right on gabbing with her girlfriend. Inside my head, my spiritual gift of sarcasm was churning out remarks I wanted to say, like: "Hey, Buffy, it's called In-N-Out, not Wait-It-Out. If I had wanted to spend this long in line, I could have ordered a burger from the DMV." I was on the verge of being mean and saying something rude. But I didn't. The only thing that kept me from it, though, was the fact that I'm a pastor and the fear that she might go to our church. Besides, if I had blown up at the gabby girl as I was tempted to, it wouldn't have solved anything, let alone gotten me my food any faster (and there may have been a mystery "extra" on my burger). Sure, she was slacking off, but the truth was, my anxious heart wasn't caused by her; it was my issue. My empty-heart issue. I was nearing empty, and it wasn't pretty. Standing in line and chewing on my fist, I knew something had to change. I got back in my car, and I stopped, prayed, apologized to God, and made a connection.

I talk to a lot of Christians who believe that living for God means not blowing it in big areas of life: committing adultery, stealing money, murder—that kind of thing. Wrong! A noncompartmentalized, fully integrated faith means obedience in the small areas too. Obedience to a managed thought life, speaking kind words, and the call to follow God's way. It's what we think at night when no one is around. It's that extra verbal jab we do (or don't) let lie when we have an argument with a friend or spouse. It's the degree to which we keep (or lose) our cool while fighting traffic or waiting in line for a burger.

Obedience is much easier when I'm living topped off and spiritually refueled.

Obedience is much easier when I'm living topped off and spiritually refueled. When my heart is full, I want to be consistent (noncompartmentalized) no matter where I am. But how do I get there? How do you?

The Fullness of Life

The idea of spiritual refueling has its roots in a strong biblical foundation. It comes from a prayer the apostle Paul prayed for the Christians at Ephesus. Paul prayed that they would be "filled to the measure of all the fullness of God" (Ephesians 3:19 NIV). But in the original language, Paul used the *present continuous* tense as he wrote this. So what was he saying, really? That he wanted the Ephesians to *be filled continuously*, or to be *filled and be filled and be filled and be filled some more*. In other words, being filled with the fullness of life doesn't happen just once. To experience the fullness of life, we need to be filled and spiritually refueled *regularly*; that is, filled and filled—and filled some more.

With that concept in mind, I want to take you on a short journey through three Scripture passages that build a strong case for being continually refueled. It's been my experience that when I know the why of something, I'm more motivated to figure out the how in the process of refueling.

We need to regularly refuel because . . .

Being *Busy* Doesn't Satisfy

In Luke 10:38–41, Jesus visits the home of two sisters, Mary and Martha. Mary enjoys connecting with Jesus, but Martha is preoccupied with the busyness of hospitality and meal preparations. When busy

Martha complains about lazy Mary, Jesus responds by saying, "Mary has chosen what is better."

This is painfully clear: connecting with Jesus is a better choice than busyness.

There will always be more to do! Know what I mean? There's a business lunch on Tuesday, soccer practice for the kids twice this week, neighbors coming over for dinner, two games on Saturday, bills piling up that need attention, an upcoming trip to the Grand Canyon that requires planning, and a to-do list that's so long that you've added "get through the to-do list" to it. There's a lot going on *now*.

So many of us are tired of rushing from one activity to the next, constantly checking schedules, arriving late, and always feeling a bit elsewhere after we arrive. There's a gnawing sense in our guts that we can't keep up the pace . . . and truth be known, we don't want to. Most people I talk to are tired of being tired all the time, tired of the emptiness that comes from too much busyness and not enough God.

Thankfully, God offers a better way than running on empty. He invites us to walk instead of run and find rest for our weary souls. That's what the fullness of life is all about. It's not the same as being busy all the time (even busy doing good things). The invitation is to sit at the feet of the Person who is the source of all fullness.

Our Souls Long to Be Filled

We need to refuel regularly, because refilling is where God provides true satisfaction—down deep, where it really matters.

When was the last time you stopped long enough to consider that you have a soul? What is your soul? If you're tempted to say, "A smooth type of music," I appreciate your answer, but it's incorrect.

Your soul is the invisible, eternal part of you, the part that connects you with God. It's what makes you different from all other life forms on the planet— every human has a soul. Your soul is the real you. That's why Jesus asked, "Is anything worth more than your soul?" (Matthew 16:26).

Jesus wanted us to understand that our souls are the most important part of who we are. We need to value, feed, and care for them.

To help you better understand, picture a balance— you know, one of those scales on which they weigh mail and packages and frozen meat and newborn iguanas (I saw that on the Discovery Channel). Imagine that one side of the scale has all the stuff you already have or are trying to gain. Tipping the scale would be all the possessions and activities you typically view as benefits—houses, cars, boats, vacations, swimming pools, stock portfolios, job titles, reputation, college degrees, iguanas, all the toys you've ever bought, and karate lessons.

Then, on the other side of the balance is simply . . . *your soul.*

It would seem obvious that the side with all the stuff should weigh down the balance, right?

Wrong!

In God's divine measuring system, stuff always loses to soul.

Jesus places a high value on your soul—it is your most valuable "possession." Because of this, your soul longs for the type of fullness whose warranty doesn't wear out after sixty days—the fullness that only God can fill through *regular connections.* And having this fullness is critical, because . . .

There's Something More Ahead

There's a fact of humanity that's often difficult to think about: *death.*

One day each of us will die—at least physically, anyway. Our hearts will cease beating. Our bodies will stop, and we'll assume room temperature. But our souls will live for eternity. We can lose a body part or have an organ transplant, but it doesn't alter the soul. Souls last. Our bodies are simply temporary containers for our souls. That's why the apostle Paul reminded us to keep an eternal perspective: "We . . . know that as long as we are at home in the body we are away from the Lord" (2 Corinthians 5:6 NIV).

By refueling, I am stashing away spiritual capital.

When we connect with God and subsequently refuel, we not only access the power and guidance we need for each day; we also invest in our eternity—our real home and final location, the place where the risen Christ is preparing for us to join Him (John 14:2–4). Being refueled is also another way to prepare me for the time when I will be entrusted with "many things" for all of eternity (Matthew 25:14–30 NIV). By refueling, I am stashing away spiritual capital that will last forever in the real adventure of being in the very presence of God.

An Uncomplicated Guide

When it comes to your soul, we need to learn how to be filled on our own at all times (rather than just one day a week while at church). If you're like me, you need a helpful, straightforward, doable way to connect with God that won't leave you paralyzed with guilt. If so, there's hope coming.

In the pages ahead, you'll learn an uncomplicated way of refueling. It's not the only way; it's one way. You'll find a way to fill up a soul that longs to be filled and to live as though you know there's Something More coming. In fact, you'll discover how to keep yourself *always topped off* so the temptation to live a compartmentalized faith won't be as strong and the pressures of daily life won't stall your spiritual engine.

The intrinsic message of what I'm suggesting isn't new—plenty of books have been written about connecting with God. What makes this one different is its simplicity. But please don't confuse simplicity with simplism. This isn't simplistic—if you learn to connect with God, it's deep. Very deep. I don't want you to try to "cram" God into an already busy schedule. Instead, I want to guide you toward a realistic way of connecting with God that is natural to your desires and the rhythm of the life you live.

Anyone can do this by practicing these three actions:

1. *Stop.*
2. *Be quiet.*
3. *Make a connection.*

Yep, that's it! It's all I'm asking you to do. This can happen in seconds or it can take hours. It's up to you. We'll go over the three actions in more depth in the following three chapters so you can see how these separate actions fit together in the refueling process—a process that can happen anywhere and at any time.

> **You're not a threat to the enemy when you're spiritually empty.**

If you're tempted to close the book after this chapter because you're thinking, *I've heard this before,* or *I've tried this—or something just like it—and it never worked before. Why would it work now?* I encourage you to rethink your hesitations. I believe excuses that may pop into your mind right now are not from God. My friend, there's a battle for your soul, and God's enemy wants you to be distracted, defeated, and empty. Why? Because you're not a threat to the enemy when you're spiritually empty. Emptiness is ineffectiveness. Empty is right where Satan wants you.

I know this simple plan can work for you. When I first taught this material to our congregation, the response was surprisingly positive. "Finally!" people said—it was as if a huge weight was lifted off their shoulders. From person after person I heard the same thing—people who had always struggled with having a stereotypical "quiet time" (the one they were sure everybody else was having much more often than they were), experienced a new type of hope. They found a pathway to fullness, and so will you.

If you're going to move forward spiritually, if you're going to experience depth and closeness to God and live out His desires for your life, if you want to experience all the fullness of life He has for you, then you must learn to regularly refuel. If that's what you want in your own life, I invite you to read on.

///////////////////////////

This Week: Take time this week to connect with someone you've chosen as a confidant in your journey toward more consistent spiritual refueling. Ask him or her to hold you accountable for what you want to practice as a result of this chapter.

Reflect: What do you think God might be saying to you after reading this chapter?

When do you feel most guilty in your relationship with God?

Write out three reasons you need to be continually refilled spiritually, and focus on the one that gives you the biggest challenge.

Prayer: Lord, You are my Creator. I thank You for wanting to connect with me and for caring about the details of my life. I want to be close to You, to experience a depth that only a growing relationship with You can bring. You've promised to give me the desires of my heart, and I want my heart to align with Yours. I want to experience all the fullness of life that You have planned for me. Please give me the strength and discipline to regularly refuel.

Stop

When was the last time you thought about the actions that go into refueling your car? I imagine it's been a long time. After doing it over and over again, refueling has become a reflex or a habit. You don't need someone to instruct you how to

1. stop at a gas station;
2. swipe your credit card;
3. squeeze the pump's handle.

Behind each action is a depth of skill and information your brain has already processed. You know, for instance, that when you stop your car at a gas station, you must apply the brakes, turn off the ignition, get out, flip open the gas cap, walk around to the pump, select the desired grade of gasoline, balk at the price, scream, wish you lived in the Middle East, consider buying an electric car, grieve, and then start refueling. You don't even need to think anymore—those actions happen automatically.

That's my goal for helping you refuel spiritually. This plan is simple, doable, and effective. After you ingest the plan and digest the information, you will train yourself to refuel on reflex. So let's start with the first action for spiritual refueling:

It's time to *stop*.

When It Spills Out

It sounds too simple.

Just *stop*.

This action is a literal invitation to bring to a halt your mind's and body's movements, to momentarily ignore responsibilities and to-do lists. It doesn't have to be a long stop . . . just stop for five minutes. Or three. Or one. Or thirty *seconds*. That's right . . . seconds! I want you to learn to create pauses in your day in order to refuel your soul. Just as you don't refuel your car while it's in motion, you can't refill your soul while you are in a flurry of activity. Being spiritually refilled requires you to *stop*.

Just as you don't refuel your car while it's in motion, you can't refill your soul while you are in a flurry of activity.

Most people find stopping very difficult when their lives have become too full. While I was writing this book, I took an informal poll of our congregation to get their pulse on this action. I asked if they could personally relate to any of the following words: *busy, rushed, empty, stressed, fatigued, overloaded*. I'd say 90 percent raised their hands, and the other 10 percent were either lying or asleep. Try it yourself. Pause for a minute to consider these words for your own life. Circle the one(s) you most identify with.

- » busy
- » rushed
- » empty
- » stressed
- » fatigued
- » overloaded

I would circle *overloaded*. There is so much to do around me, just waiting to be embraced, and I'm ever reminded of it. Right now, on an electronic device smaller than a candy bar, I can check and send e-mail, take pictures and record video, receive sports scores, download stock market news, watch movie previews, and collect much of the world's information. I have more data swarming around me today than all the kings of centuries past. A hundred years ago mail traveled for weeks on horseback. Now it zips around the globe in nanoseconds. Today's delivery systems provide me with more speed, information, affluence, education, and entertainment than any previous generation experienced. It can all be overwhelming. I feel overloaded right now just writing about it.

How can you tell if stopping would be too difficult for you? I'm sure there are many ways, but most people describe a busy life as a life with no margins. You know what margins are—in a spiral notebook they are those blank white spaces on the sides of each page. Margin is space without activity.

It is my observation that a life without margins is a life in or rapidly approaching chaos. A marginless day is crammed with running, driving, chasing, little time to catch your breath, and limited time to think something through or even to decompress. If that describes you, you're most likely an accident waiting to happen.

A life without margins is a life in or rapidly approaching chaos.

One of the strongest indicators of a packed life is when your reactions to circumstances don't match the reality of the moment—in other words, when your emotions get the best of you. Recently I pulled into a parking space at one of my favorite "fine-dining" restaurants, Burgers & Donuts. (I'm not making this name up. Google it.) At the same time, a well-dressed, fortysomething woman in a white Chevy Suburban pulled into the space next to me. As I opened my door, I accidentally touched my car door to her door. It didn't make any dent—just a tiny *tink* sound. The woman went ballistic. By her reaction, you'd have thought I had taken my car keys and scrawled "I hate Chevy Suburbans and you" on her door. Out of her mouth spewed the foulest language I've ever heard. She didn't just drop the F-bomb—she dropped A- through Z-bombs too. I've never even heard of some of the words she used (I learned stuff about my mom that I never knew before). I apologized and assured her there was no damage. She didn't want to listen. Instead, she returned to her car, slammed the door, displayed the international sign of displeasure, and roared away without a burger or a donut or a conversation.

I'm not sure what was happening in that woman's life, but she definitely had an out-of-proportion reaction. When you're worn-out, you have no emotional reserves available for when you are "tinked." It doesn't matter if it's a grocery store line that's too long, a pair of socks left on a child's bedroom floor, or a coworker's cell phone that incessantly rings to the tune of "Macarena." When there is no margin, the slightest thing can set us off. We blow up, then wonder what just happened.

Why is it, with all of these luxuries, technologies, and time-saving devices in our lives, that we're still busy, tired, and marginless? I believe it's because a series of lies has barged in and taken root in our lives. If we are ever to experience margins, we must do a little digging to uproot the untruths and expose them for what they really are. Let's consider a few and see why it's so difficult to stop.

LIE: There's just not enough time to do everything.

No "time fairy" is going to sprinkle magic dust on our lives and give us an extra three hours a day. The truth is, there is always enough time to do what God wants us to do. Too often the real reason we feel as though there's not enough time is because we've either mismanaged our time and priorities or filled our day with trivial activities. Today I wanted to go by my mom's house for a short visit, but instead of doing that, I got enthralled with an infomercial for a hair care product that I can't afford and would never use anyway. It was interesting yet trivial, and before I knew it, I had to get to a school event for my kids, and I missed visiting her. I had the time; I just misused it (please don't tell my mom).

Jesus' life shows us that a person can do all he was meant to do in the time allotted for him. Jesus said yes to many things, but He also said no to many other things. Jesus set boundaries. He had limits. When the demands upon Him became too great, and He found Himself physically and spiritually depleted, He withdrew "to a mountain by himself" (John 6:15 NIV) or "by boat privately to a solitary place" (Matthew 14:13

NIV). He recognized that He needed time to stop, reflect, pray, and nourish His inner life. So do we.

LIE: I'm just in a busy season right now.

Sure, there are busy seasons in life. Final exam week in college. The months following a newborn. A few days before an important deadline at work. The problem is that it's too convenient to use this statement to characterize *every* month, week, and day.

Personally, this is the lie I often return to. A true busy season comes to an end, but another busy season blends into yet another busy season, and the pressure never seems to lighten up. I always say that less busy times are around the corner, but they never arrive.

Truthfully, it's often not the season that's busy; it's the person. It's me. "Busy-addicts" search for opportunities to score their drug of choice—activity. This is a tough lie to stop believing.

LIE: But this is really, really important.

When you believe this lie, you say yes to everything. Whatever opportunities come your way, you pile them on your plate. Other people's issues have a way of becoming your problems. Other people's crises become your urgencies. It's all worthwhile stuff, you tell yourself, and you're convinced that if you didn't say yes, then all that worthwhile stuff wouldn't get done.

I'll let you in on a little secret: it's okay to say no. You can't do everything, nor should you. If you don't believe me, ask Dan Cathy, president and COO of Chick-fil-A, one of the largest privately owned fast-food chains in the United States.

One day I had the privilege of having lunch with Dan, and during our meal, I made a presentation for a book idea that I wanted to coauthor with him. I ended my pitch with, "I imagine you are so busy, and this is just another idea fighting for your time, but I thought I'd ask anyway." What he said in response really stuck with me.

"Doug," he answered, "I *am* busy. I'm very busy. But even busy people find time for what they believe is really important. But not everything can be and is important." That was a great concept that I needed to hear and apply!

That book has never been written, so that tells you what Dan thought of my idea. Or maybe it was a good idea that is still standing in a long line of good ideas waiting for an opportunity within a schedule that allows for margin. But Dan Cathy knows that everything isn't really, really important, and that was refreshing to see from a man of his status.

LIE: Success and busyness are synonyms.

Ever notice how easy it is to treat busyness as a badge of honor? Say you run into a friend you haven't seen in a while. The exchange might sound like this:

"Hey, how are you doing? Stayin' busy?"

"Oh, I'm slammed! You?"

"Yep, totally in over my head!"

"Yeah, me too. Can't believe the season we're in right now at work."

"I hear you. Who needs sleep?"

"Glad to hear you're doing well!"

"Yeah, you too. Congratulations!"

Doing *well*? Really? Is being busy truly good? In the eyes of many, busyness is sexy. Busyness is a sign that you're something. People need you. You're important. You've arrived.

Wait, that's the lie. Do you see it?

I have a good friend who has bought into this lie and is always busy at work and is rarely home. As a buddy, I felt I could confront him on this situation. He listened, but he became defensive and said, "Doug, I've got to stay busy to pay the bills." I believe that part of his problem is that he has a lot of unnecessary bills that are more tied to status and success than survival. He recently bought his wife a brand-new Hummer. He said he purchased the expensive vehicle because it was "safe." I'm skeptical. He has also chosen to live in a neighborhood that is above his means, where he can show off his overpriced military artillery vehicle—which he doesn't really need. So was he telling the truth when he said he was "staying busy to pay the bills"? Oh yeah. He was also busy supporting poor choices that made him feel successful.

In the eyes of many, busyness is sexy. Busyness is a sign that you're something.

This type of living is killing people. It's destroying marriages, crippling families, shriveling hearts, and eating away at the ability to experience the fullness of life.

How about your life? Do you wish you could pull back on the throttle of your schedule? If so, the solution is to confront the lies and stop justifying busyness. Stopping may feel abrupt at first, but it's a necessary ingredient in the refueling recipe.

When my youngest daughter, Cassie, was about three years old, I was holding her while talking with someone after church. She was struggling in my arms, trying to get my attention, but I remained focused on my conversation. Finally, Cassie grabbed both sides of my face with her two hands and said, "Daddy— stop. *Stop!* Stop talking, and look at me!" She forced my attention.

That's what I want to do with you. I want to grab you by the face (gently) and give you this abrupt message: *Stop!*

Stop saying yes to everything.

Stop occupying your life with trivial things.

Stop filling your life with too many good things and living a busy life with no margins and no space for God and what really matters.

Stop so you can refuel your soul and have the spiritual depth to battle the superficiality of busyness.

A "Cessation" Plan

If your life is stuffed with busyness, my invitation for you today is *not* to stop everything and radically alter your life. That may sound strange to you, but I'm not asking you to set down this book, pull your kids out of soccer practice, quit your job, sell your Hummer, or get up three hours earlier every morning. My plan is serious, yes—it's serious enough to make me want to grab your cheeks and scream, "Stop!"—but it is also well within reach. This is a plan you can succeed at today.

When you try to imagine what *stop* means for you, I don't want you to feel pressure to move to backwoods Montana to escape everything. When some folks envision their lives slowing down, they fantasize about a dreamy, tranquil place where they enjoy quiet times, sitting on a huge porch overlooking a big lawn, with hummingbirds hovering and deer playfully prancing. There's an open Bible on their lap, a cup of perfectly brewed coffee nearby, and a stack of note cards with Scripture verses handwritten in calligraphy. They can even see the Lord Himself mysteriously appearing from the shrubbery to wave hi. Spectacular! It's a nice fantasy, but it's not reality. I'm not asking you to chase that dream. My invitation is for you to connect with God while living in the real world. The type of stopping I'm suggesting is meant to be liberating. I want to puncture the guilt-laden images of quiet times you know you'll never have. I'm not inviting you to spend hours on your knees, or study Scripture in the original Greek, or sit down after every meal with your family and sing "Kumbaya" before memorizing the entire book of Psalms. My appeal is for you to stop within your normal schedule. Simply allow for small margins of "stop" in the midst of daily life. I want you to learn how to create pauses—each day, several times a day—when you can stop, become quiet, and connect with God. I believe that the more often you do this, the more aware you'll become of your pace and level of busyness. Connecting with God will help you make wiser decisions.

Stop *within* your normal schedule.

I know you can do it. Now let's just make it practical:

» Stopping can be as simple as arriving at a meeting five minutes ahead of time and sitting outside the conference room with enough time to handwrite a prayer.

» Stopping can be getting into your car for

your commute to work with two minutes to spare between clicking your seat belt and starting the engine, using the time to read your Bible, then thinking about what you just read as you drive.

» Stopping can be turning off your computer at the end of the day and sitting completely still at your desk for a short pause of prayer before grabbing your briefcase and heading out the door.

» Stopping can be as easy as shutting the refrigerator (or finishing any task) and walking into another room for a minute of reflection.

» Stopping can happen in the middle of a busy grocery store. Or while waiting to pick up your child after school. Or while using the bathroom (I told you this would be a practical book).

Stopping isn't designed to be just one more activity to add to your already-too-full life. It is simply allowing space around an activity so you can focus on God. Try it for one day. Then two. Find consistency in a couple of stops before you add a third one. You guessed it: when you're consistent at three stops, look for a fourth opportunity. Soon, stopping will become habitual. This is crucial, because taking the time to stop enables you to purposely create small yet significant margins in your life. These minimargins add up to larger moments of stop. You can refuel your soul and keep it topped off with several small, daily stops. But you cannot get or stay topped off if you don't have any margin in which to stop.

Start slow. If you're out of shape physically, you wouldn't begin exercising by attempting a marathon. You'd be out of steam in half a mile. Instead, you would start with a walk around the block. A jog to the corner and back. A short sprint followed by a longer walk. Basically, you work up to it. That's my suggestion with regard to stopping too. You may actually need to learn how to stop.

Here's an example of a small stop I made a few minutes ago. Yesterday a friend gave me one of those electronic devices that you wear on your arm to calculate the number of calories you expend throughout the day. It came with a free phone consultation with one of the company's fitness coaches—which I wasn't interested in. I was fairly confident that the free fitness consultation was actually going to be a sales pitch, pressuring me to buy vitamins and supplements I didn't want. But in order to get my gizmo activated, I needed to include my phone number on an online form. Sure enough, today I got a phone call. But I chose not to take the call. I was tempted to answer, but I didn't. By not taking the call, I created a margin. Here's the result: I traded twenty minutes on the phone with a stranger for an extended stop to spend time with my Savior. That was the right choice, and while it may not be revolutionary, it's exactly that type of normal moment in my life when I can be refilled, moments when I've chosen to say no to create a margin so I can stop and say yes to God.

Please understand that I'm not suggesting you give God your leftovers.

Please understand that I'm not suggesting you give God your leftovers. Certainly there are times when we are able to spend large amounts of time with God—extended periods of prayer, spiritual retreats, weekly Bible study sessions—and I welcome those times in my own life and recommend them in yours. But the focus of this book isn't on those larger times. Those stops will happen naturally when you master the smaller times.

Without looking too hard, I can always find small, realistic slivers of time during which I can stop, be quiet, and connect with God. I find them every day, several times a day. And when God and I regularly connect, my focus is clearer, my perspective is brighter, my joy is richer, and I experience more of the fullness of life that God offers.

That's spiritual refueling. And it can happen in your life too.

An Invitation to Be Still

If stopping is a new idea to you, it may feel unusual when you first put it into practice. That's okay. Remember the first time you learned how to dive into a swimming pool? Chances are it turned into a belly flop, or you jumped in feet first—with your hands in a diving position. Diving? No. Dorky? Yes. But it became easier and more natural over time.

Everything worth doing requires some learning and a bit of adjustment. Stopping may feel uncomfortable at first. It may even feel drastic. But just as you learned to dive off that board years ago by taking those first few steps, you can learn to do this. Be warned, though: the busier you are, the more difficult stopping will be. Yet you can do it! I know you can.

Consider this moment your invitation to stop. Sit down and empty your brain of your to-do lists and tasks. Right now, stop your body's motion. Bring your busy mind to an abrupt halt, your hurried spirit to a standstill. Stop *everything*. Just stop. Heed the advice of the famous psalm: "Be still, and know that I am God" (46:10 NIV).

That's what it means to stop. To be still. To cease activity and consciously focus your thoughts on God. Don't rush to the next chapter . . . instead, stop. Put this book down. Pause. You can't refuel your soul if you're always moving.

Stop.

///////////////////////

This week: Take notice of what fills the small spaces of your life and write them down. Keep a record for one week of specific times you made an effort to stop. Don't evaluate that stop, just stop. At the end of a week, write down your observations.

Reflect: What do you think God might be saying to you after reading this chapter?

What needs to change in your life so you can stop and slow down?

Prayer: Lord, my life often feels overloaded, and I'm pulled in so many directions. I'm frequently much too busy for my own good. I've been worn out and exhausted, and I know that isn't Your desire for me. Help me to remember that You created us to run at the pace You designed, a pace that will allow me to connect regularly with You. Help me to see and focus on the things that are important to You. Help me to stop and learn to create and value margin in my life.

Be Quiet

I will never forget the day I came home from work to find my wife *hiding* in the bathroom. Our kids were ages six, three, and six months. It wasn't Cathy's parenting style to medicate the children to quiet them down—or medicate *herself* to pursue quiet. She was simply in a desperate search for noiselessness. There have been many days in her life as Mommy when she has longed for a slice of silence. There's just something so necessary about quiet.

Connecting with God involves another radical action besides "stop." It's an essential ingredient in the recipe of spiritual growth—quiet. Immediately after you create a *pause*, I want to also encourage you to find *silence* . . . hopefully without having to hide in the bathroom.

In a world where noise is everywhere, silence can seem deafening. So how do you simply *be quiet* when noise is always present, cranked up to high volume? Think about all the noise that is around you whether you want it or not. All day long you experience noise: commuting noise, human noise, media noise, advertising noise, disaster noise, advice noise, shopping noise, reality-TV noise—so much clatter that it even forces the noise level to *rise* in order to hear or be heard. Even if we try to escape the racket by going for a walk, there's a temptation to put on earphones and bring in more noise. Then, at the end of the day, we resort to playing nature sounds (more noise) next to our beds to help us fall asleep. Does this seem psycho to you? Have you ever taken the time to pay attention to the specific noises in your life?

When sound is muted, the resulting quiet forces us to think, reflect, examine our inner lives. Actually, that's why many people tend to like noise—looking inward can often take us to a lonely, dark, and difficult place. Silence has a way of forcing thought toward areas we'd rather not face. So by keeping our lives turned up loud, we don't have to deal with the realities of life that hide in the quiet.

But it's in silence—the absence of noise—where God often reveals Himself. In silence God doesn't compete for attention with ESPN or CSI. In quietness, God can guide us, direct us, surround us with His presence and love. But before we can clearly hear the voice of God addressed to our hearts, finding silence is essential.

It's in silence—the absence of noise—where God often reveals Himself.

As with my challenge to *stop* in the last chapter, I'm not asking you to seek out large segments of silence. There are times and places for those. But I do want you to learn to find slivers of silence in your daily routine. I want you to get comfortable with *choosing* quiet.

The challenge of being quiet involves more than simply shutting yourself off from what you can hear. That's because "noise" is not limited to what comes into our ears; it's also what swirls about in our minds, those silent distractions that cause our minds to stay active and unfocused on God.

Noise Without Sound

Let's look at a few enemies of silence. These "noises" are not audible, but they are noisy nonetheless. They are, in fact, the "biggies," those things that turn up the volume in the chamber of a heart that needs quiet to connect with God. See if any of these are making noise in your life.

Worry

Worry can shout at you. It can wake you up in the middle of the night and fill your heart with dread. It can make you nervous before a day begins. It can fill your mind and your conversations and even occupy your times of relaxation.

It's easy to worry. Give me a subject—anything— and I can worry about it. Even something as innocuous as baseball. *What if my DVR doesn't record the game? What if I hear the score before I get home to watch it? What if there are no buffalo wings left in the fridge? What if a foul ball causes an old lady to trip? What if that old lady is my mom?* I could go on and on.

Worry is an ever-present shout. That's why Jesus urged us to keep things in perspective. "Who of you by worrying can add a single hour to his life?" He asked (Luke 12:25 NIV; see verses 22–31 for context). Worry is the opposite of worship. It's a noise that's difficult to extinguish.

Want

The noise of wanting can be deafening. It's rough to find silence if you have a consumption mentality. You're always thinking about more. So you buy and buy and buy—all in an attempt to "buy" serenity. If you're worried or stressed or angry or bored, it's so easy to drive to the mall and attempt to purchase peace. It's second nature. You're simply responding to the inner noise of wanting. But where does it come from to begin with?

It screams from both impersonal sources, such as advertisements, and personal sources—our own friends and families. We flip through magazines and notice how good the gadgets look on those glossy pages, and we think about them all day. Or we notice that our neighbor has just bought himself a new SUV, and we ache for one too. A colleague returns to the office, tanned from a Tahiti vacation, and we get itchy to call a travel agent. We're overwhelmed by the silent-but-earsplitting scream of desire. It convinces us that in order to look good, feel good, or be good, we need something we *don't have*. The solution to all of our problems is just one purchase away.

Sometimes we buy for our personal use, and what we pay for, we actually need. But *sometimes* we buy simply in an attempt to grasp a moment's peace. Example? Buying your son a drum set—to keep him from bugging *you*. Does it help? No. But it does leave you hard of hearing. And meanwhile, it doesn't satisfy your son anyway. Why? Because he's just like you—and me, marching to the drumbeat of *I want* MORE. The noise of wanting is both cacophonous *and* contagious.

Procrastination

Procrastination creates a strange noise. Whenever we put something off that we could (or should) do today, a dull, droning voice nags at us incessantly. Meanwhile, we add to the noise as we, in effect, put our fingers in our ears and run around singing, "La la la," ignoring a situation in hopes that it will resolve itself or disappear.

The effects of procrastination become louder over

time. Clutter builds up in our lives. Unresolved relationships fester in the back of our minds. Things left unsaid, tasks left undone, situations left unhandled—it all adds up and looms in the recesses of our minds. Soon the nagging din caused by our own procrastination can reach fingernails-on-chalkboard levels.

The Noise All Around You

Let's take a short self-inventory of the current noise level in your life. Take a minute to write down the letter (A, B, C) that best corresponds to the following statements. This survey isn't meant to be scientific, but it will provide you an opportunity for self-reflection. You may want to talk through the results with your small group or a trusted friend.

A = rarely
B = sometimes
C = most of the time

_____ I listen to music throughout the day.
_____ My evenings are filled with watching television or doing stuff on the computer.

_____ I need music or the radio on whenever I'm in the car.

_____ I talk a lot. It doesn't really matter to whom or where. On the phone. To coworkers. Really everyone I meet.

_____ The TV is on most of the time at our house, even though no one is really watching it.

_____ I buy things to feel better, or when I'm angry, depressed, or bored.

_____ I wake up from sleep worried.

_____ There are conversations that I know I need to have, but I've been putting them off.

_____ My life is usually "noisy."

_____ I feel most comfortable when there's noise.

Score yourself.

» For each **A** you wrote, score yourself **0 decibels**.

» For each **B** you wrote, score yourself **5 decibels**.

» For each **C** you wrote, score yourself **10 decibels**.

Now add up your decibels. How did you do?

0–35 decibels. *Rustle-of-leaves level.* Congratulations! Your life appears to have a level of silence to it. You've succeeded at turning down the volume of worry, consumption, and procrastination, as well as overt noise in your life. Set down this book and give yourself a pat on the back. Or be really honest and take the test again.

40–65 decibels. *Conversation level.* Not bad. Your life may be characterized by periods of both volume and silence. It sounds as if you're aware of the dangers of worry, consumption, and procrastination, as well as too much overt noise in your life, and you've taken some steps to combat these. Good job.

70–100 decibels. *Jackhammer level.* Danger zone. Your life is over-the-top loud. There is little silence in your day. Sometimes your life feels jittery and chaotic. In honest moments of reflection, you see some rough spots in your inner life that you don't really want to face. Left unchecked, the noise in your life will increase and continue to drown out the voice of God.

If you're like most people, you scored in the second or third group. So what's the solution?

The Whisper Voice

The solution is to pursue quiet.

It's that simple . . . and apparently that complex too.

You don't have to become a monk and stay mute for a year. You don't have to enclose your house in insulating bubble wrap. You don't even have to burn your rock 'n' roll CDs on your front lawn or destroy your TV. Instead, after each "stop" you create throughout the day, just allow yourself to be quiet. Consciously choose no noise. Clear out the noise of worry. Turn off the clamor of consumption. Silence the noise of procrastination. Quiet your life in small ways. Doable. Practical. Attainable. Even undersized times of quiet will add up and bring big rewards.

What happens when we're quiet? We are more apt to hear the voice of God, for God often speaks through silence. Many of us look for the voice of God in the *events*—the weekly sermon, praise music at church, large-scale worship gatherings, spiritual seminars and conferences that come to town. But it's also in the small moments each day where God may be speaking. Maybe in a time of silence, a name comes to mind, and we know we need to go to that person and reconcile a hurt. Or perhaps in the quiet, a specific situation—one that requires confession—suggests itself. When there is silence, we may even hear the voice of God saying, "I love you" through His creation (such as a rosy-hued sunset, a flower, or a pristine mountain).

I realize that the thought of God speaking may be mind stretching. While God's voice is not audible—at least I've never heard it that way—it is recognizable. It's a different type of voice that can be heard as a gentle leading, a specific prompting, or what might be called an impression that's "heard" in your heart.

He loves you so much; why wouldn't He want to guide you?

God is not distant. He communicates through His Spirit. He loves you so much; why wouldn't He want to guide you? John 16:13 says that the Holy Spirit guides us into all truth—that's one of the roles of God's Spirit dwelling in a life. This guidance can happen through an impression in your heart, or you can hear God's voice in the pages of Scripture. The Holy Spirit may open your heart to hear God's unique and personal application through a Bible verse. You're reading along, and all of a sudden a word or a phrase becomes really clear or relatable in a unique way. You've read it before, but this time is different. You know it's for you. Could that be God's voice? I think so.

God also communicates to us through people. Sometimes it's as obvious as a pastor giving a message at church, and you feel as if it is for you and only you. But other times God's voice is subtler (and easy to miss).

One of my favorite God-moments happened right before I was about to preach at my church. On this day I was particularly stressed-out and nervous. Actually, I often feel that way before I teach. On the way to church, I stopped by a grocery store to buy throat lozenges. Once inside, I saw someone I knew was going through difficult times, but I was too preoccupied with my own agenda to want to talk. It's embarrassing to admit, but I looked the other way and pretended not to notice him.

Once I got into my car, I stopped for a brief moment, before racing off to church, to reflect on what had just happened. (I was practicing the process I'm suggesting in this book—stop, be quiet, make a connection.) Instantly I felt convicted about ignoring an opportunity to care for someone through conversation. I wondered if God was prompting me to go back into the store, find the person I knew, and apologize for my selfishness.

And then a funny thing happened. Sitting there, I sensed a very strong leading to stay in my car. It wasn't audible, but very clearly I sensed these words: *Stay here . . . Be still.* (This happened in seconds, not minutes.)

As I sat in my car, wondering if there was more to the leading, I saw an elderly woman come out of the store. She was wrestling with groceries, a demon-possessed shopping cart, and her purse. Before she got to her car, she dropped her purse, and there was an immediate evacuation of everything she had stuffed in it since at least the Great Depression. I think I even saw Confederate money float to the ground. I quickly got out of my car and began gathering her items. I thought, *Okay, God, this is why I stayed here—to be the hero and help her.* As I returned her possessions, I noticed a cross hanging from her necklace. When I see one, I always wonder if the owner really knows the meaning behind the symbol. This elderly woman looked at me with calm and grateful eyes and uttered a line I'll never forget: "It's going to be all right. God loves you!" She wasn't worried about herself at all. She was telling me it was going to be all right, when she was the one who should have been freaking out that the contents of her portable storage unit were flying all over the parking lot. Maybe it was the way she said it, the calmness and wisdom in her voice—I wish I could convey on paper the exact inflection she used, but I can't. What's important is that God was using this sweet saint to say, *It's going to be all right, Doug. I love you.* Then she was gone.

Those words were for me. I've always battled fear and stress prior to preaching at my church. I hate the battle. God knows that, and so, in all His sovereignty, He chose that circumstance for me to hear His voice. Driving to the church, I felt a real sense of peace and God's presence. But then, when I pulled into the parking lot, I realized that I'd never gone back into the store to talk to the guy I'd seen. And the guilt came back.

Oh well . . . at least I'm confident God loves me.

Now I focus on those words every weekend when

I get up to speak. When I'm feeling stressed, inadequate, and fearful, I recall the words of God spoken through a frail and clumsy messenger: *It's going to be all right. God loves you.*

I know that God's whisper to "stay" wasn't an accident.

The Quietness You Don't Hear

One of my favorite displays of the voice of God is found in the story of an Old Testament prophet named Elijah. Elijah did a lot of over-the-top, amazing things for God, but one day he got scared, overwhelmed, and tried to run away. After defying evil kings, slaughtering false prophets, and running a marathon to flee for his life, Elijah found himself in the wilderness, praying desperate prayers to God. His prayers were answered. God heard Elijah, strengthened his frame, then led him on a journey to a mountaintop to hear His voice. But God's voice came in a way Elijah never expected.

> Then he [Elijah] was told, "Go, stand on the mountain at attention before GOD. GOD will pass by."

A hurricane wind ripped through the mountains and shattered the rocks before GOD, but GOD wasn't to be found in the wind; after the wind an earthquake, but GOD wasn't in the earthquake; and after the earthquake fire, but GOD wasn't in the fire; and after the fire a *gentle and quiet whisper*.

When Elijah heard the quiet voice, he muffled his face with his great cloak, went to the mouth of the cave, and stood there. (1 Kings 19:11–13 MSG, emphasis added)

I love thinking about God's voice that way. His voice wasn't found in the noise. Not in the roar of the wind. Not in the chaos of an earthquake. Not in the crackles of the fire. The voice of God came in a whisper. Specifically, a "gentle and quiet" whisper.

I often wonder how many times I've missed God's personalized whisper because there has been too much noise in my life for me to hear His soft voice. What about you? Could noise be drowning out God's words directed to you?

If so, let me offer some practical thoughts on what it means to be quiet. We are real people who live in a modern-day world of traffic jams, kids' sports practices, and information coming at us from every angle. Yet we can learn to find and appreciate quiet, even in noisy environments, and learn to listen for the voice of God.

I want to encourage you, as much as you can, to work to unplug your life—certainly during specific moments throughout the day, but as a long-term strategy as well. One spiritual discipline mentioned in the Bible is fasting—an extended absence of food. Fasting is giving up food in order to gain time to focus on God. But since it's designed to create a change of focus, what about trying a fast from noise? Turn off the radio, the news, the strange, the disturbing, the loud. Try it for just an hour at first. No TV, no phone, no newspapers, no Internet. See what happens . . . I'm guessing you'll live. After you survive an hour and taste something different, try it again. Do it often. Train yourself to long for quiet, and grab it when you can

Try turning off your mobile phone. I've made it a practice to keep my phone turned off during all meals. I was challenged by a friend who said, "Are you so indispensable to the orbiting pattern of the earth that you can't turn off your phone and be inaccessible during certain times of the day? Let voice mail pick up your calls. You don't always have to be connected. You have that choice." He was right, and it has been a good move for me.

Do you want a quieter life? These two words may help: *power button.*

Do you want a quieter life? These two words may help: *power button.* Figure out a way to turn it off—whatever electronic device is making noise and demanding your attention—at least occasionally. I'm not suggesting you become Amish and run away from electricity, but I know from experience that a quieter life requires radical actions. Maybe that means more than turning off your phone during meals. How about keeping it off during church, during prayer, and when you're spending time with significant people in your life? Here are a few other baby steps that may not be as painful as limiting your phone time:

» Learn to fall asleep without noise.
» Turn off the radio when you get in the car (at least sometimes).
» Wake up to an alarm that you turn off rather

than a radio station that you listen to while you get ready.

» Do your housework without any electronic background noise.
» Take a walk or a jog without wearing headphones.
» Establish a no-noise room or a noise-free time zone within your home.

You can do it, right now, this moment. I know you can! Take five minutes and stop the noise. Don't go on to another task. Just turn off the noise and consciously be quiet. Walk to another room. Go outside if needed. Don't put on the headphones. Don't pick up the newspaper or flip on the TV. Instead, deliberately focus your thoughts away from the distractions of the day and move them toward God.

When the noise is gone, be prepared to connect with God.

///////////////////////

This Week: Seek out opportunities to get quiet. Turn your mobile phone off for an hour. Keep the television set, radio or laptop off for one evening.

Reflect: What do you think God might be saying to you after reading this chapter?

Where is the most noise currently the loudest in your life? What may need to change for you to enjoy quiet?

Prayer: Lord, I know You will always be there when I am able quiet my heart and come to You. I know You are waiting to connect with me. Help me to be comfortable in the silence and actively pursue quiet moments in my life. Help me to hear Your personalized whisper, the words You are speaking to me and me alone. Lord, speak to me now . . .

Make a Connection

My oldest daughter, Torie, has broken my heart by moving out of the house and living in a college dorm. I'm thrilled for her and yet sad for the rest of the family. Her move has required a greater adjustment than I ever realized. I miss her so much! But it has become easier to deal with her absence because we stay in constant contact via text messaging. Even though the messages are cryptic, they provide just enough connection to keep my heart full.

You've seen the shorthand abbreviations used in text messaging—IDK means "I don't know," TTYL means "talk to you later," LOL means "laugh[ing] out loud," YLMMTMR means "you like me more than Mom, right?"—stuff like that. Your thumbs don't have a lot of room on the tiny phone keyboards, so everything becomes quicker, more compressed, and sloppy. Today I took ten seconds to text my daughter the words "Psalm 18:30." Torie texted back, "Thanks. I love you, Dad!" Her text made an immediate impression on my heart. I don't even know if she took time to read the verse, but her connection was so meaningful.

Sometimes my wife will ask, "Have you talked to Torie today?"

"Yes," I'll reply. "She got a B on her psychology test, she's studying at Denny's with Lindsey, and then she's going to the basketball game with Delia. Seems like she's doing great."

Cathy will usually follow up with, "When did you talk to her?" I then have to admit that I didn't even hear her voice, because our connections were through texting. A simple text message allows us to stay emotionally connected without requiring us to be audible.

If anyone understands small snippets of connection, it's our current generation. We're constantly linked to others through e-mail, texting, instant messaging, Skype, Twitter, mobile phones, BlackBerrys, blueberries, strawberries—connecting with others is an integral part of who we are, and even when done quickly, it can be done *authentically*.

Likewise, quick, heartfelt connections with God can be authentic, and they can keep your soul full. God doesn't judge the connection. It's okay even if it's messy, speedy, and comes in short bites. Your heavenly Father loves to connect . . . contact brings Him joy.

As a reminder, I'm advocating a series of small pauses every day, when you stop, become quiet, and then connect with God. Nothing huge. No getting up at 4:00 a.m. for hours of prayer and Bible reading. Just small, daily snippets of refueling connections that become habitual and lead to your spiritual tank being filled. God is the One who refuels you spiritually, and when you live life with a full spiritual tank, you can experience *all* of the fullness of life that God promises.

A Messy Faith

Living the full life God desires for you doesn't mean you will look perfect all the time. You're not perfect, but because of your regular connections, you'll be moving toward consistency and intimacy with God. I describe my spiritual life as growing but still messy. Would that work for you too? I think it's a pretty fair description of most followers of Jesus.

God isn't surprised by our messiness (sin) and actually meets it with an amazing gift called grace. Grace acknowledges that there will be times when we say or do inappropriate things. Grace understands the spiritual commitments we don't keep. It recognizes that we will lose our patience, make dumb mistakes, follow through with bad choices, and think evil thoughts. Grace keeps us going and growing.

The apostle Paul lived an incredibly messy life. He knew it, too. He said, "When I try not to do wrong, I do it anyway" (see Romans 7:15–19). I can relate to that! Thankfully, the Bible is overflowing with other messy people like Paul. The flaws of biblical heroes are not edited out of the Bible. Only preachers tidy up biblical flaws. For instance, we hear about Noah's faithfulness, courage, and strength, about how he built an ark in the middle of nowhere and followed God with all his heart. He was obedient! But keep reading. The sordid part is in Genesis 9:20–27. Once Noah left the boat, he planted a vineyard, drank till he was soused, got naked . . . and everything got ugly. Why leave that out?

Noah is a model of faithfulness? Yep! The Bible reveals that even the strong and faithful have downsides. All of the biblical characters were a complex mix of strengths and weaknesses and in need of grace—just like you and me.

Our messiness leads to holiness.

Let me be clear. Grace doesn't mean that God gives a big thumbs-up to our faults, sinful hearts, and unbiblical living. He doesn't condone our messiness. Sin is an ugly act of disobedience to God's ways. But we all do it. We have all fallen short of God's ideal (Romans 3:23). But when we give our messiness to God, He redeems it. That's the real gift of grace! God doesn't encourage us to screw up; He saves us after we screw up. God takes all our sin and, over time, completely transforms us into holiness. God isn't just into fine-tuning our manners. He wants to renovate our total character. The writer of Hebrews lays it on the line: "What God wants is for us to be made holy" (10:10). That can only be accomplished if we are willing to connect with God. Once we do, and we make it a customary and recurrent priority, our messiness leads to holiness.

A theological term for God making us holy is *sanctification*. Sanctification is a beautiful and empowering gift that, when dissected, is God saying, "I love you. I love you so much that I don't want you to stay the same. And because I love you, I'm going to take your sin and change your messiness into something great." The essence of this teaching is found in 2 Corinthians 3:18: "We are transfigured much like the Messiah, our lives *gradually* becoming brighter and more beautiful as God enters our lives and we become like him" (MSG, emphasis added).

When you understand what God wants to do in your life (did you notice the word *gradually* in the verse?), who He wants you to become, and how He wants to connect with you and transform your messiness into holiness, it can drive you closer to Him. Because I know what God wants for me, I'm highly motivated to connect with Him.

When We Connect with God

If you feel spiritually messy, you're in good company. Hopefully that's a theme that you've felt throughout the book: *You're not alone.* Yet in spite of your sinful nature, you get to be a beneficiary of God's transforming power. Transformation is something only He can do. God does His part; you do your part. Thankfully, our part is so easy to remember: *stop*, *be quiet*, and *connect*.

Let's consider what a connection might look like. We'll begin with some broad strokes and then move to some specific ideas. I want to be very clear that the actual actions you use to connect to God are much less important than the attitude of your heart. Connecting with God isn't about mastering a formula; it's about a heart that desires to be closer to God. It's an attitude that acknowledges who He is, the King of kings. You come to God with reverence, respect, and admiration, but you also draw near confidently, knowing that He is approachable and you will receive the grace you need when you connect with Him (Hebrews 4:16).

When you connect with God, consider taking the following broad actions.

Thank God That You're Under Construction

When we connect with God, we do so knowing that we're not perfect, but God is. God is fully aware of our emotional and spiritual disarray and the certainty

that we're works in progress. A perfect response to
this reality is gratefulness.

**When we connect with God, we do so knowing
that we're not perfect, but God is.**

I am so thankful that I don't fall under a spiritual
rule similar to the "three strikes" crime law that
governs California, where I live. That law says that if
you get convicted three times, you go to jail for
life—regardless of the crimes. Can you imagine if
God had a "three strikes" rule for you? You can't go
to heaven if you've disobeyed God's ways three
times? All the churches in the world would be
empty. In my state, you get three strikes and you'll
end up with what you deserve—you get the law. But
in God's state, when you mess up, you get what you
don't *deserve*—you get *grace*.

Remember the old bumper sticker that read
"Please be patient. God isn't finished with me yet"?
That's more than cliché; that's good theology. God
isn't done with you (remember *sanctification*, on page
80?). Your new life begins with Christ (2 Corinthians
5:17) and then remains under construction until
you're in His presence in eternity.

God is at work on our lives. Construction will never be fully finished this side of heaven. There will always be some sort of mess God is working with. But every time we notice a positive change in our character, we can thank God because He's at work.

Trust God in Your Unfinishedness

You may not like the fact that God doesn't work faster in your life—or the way you think He should. But when you connect with God, you are trusting that He has a master plan in mind for you, worked out in the midst of a journey filled with fears, doubts, questions, failures, inadequacies, pain, loneliness, anger, frustration, and loss. In spite of failure, we trust that the God who began the good work will continue it. Listen to these strong words of trust: "God, who began the good work within you, will continue his work until it is finally finished on that day when Christ Jesus comes back again" (Philippians 1:6).

God has a wonderful track record of working behind the scenes in spite of messiness. When you read the book of 1 Corinthians, you see a bunch of Christ-followers dealing with incestuous affairs, vicious lawsuits, divorce, idol worship, inflated egos, doctrinal infighting, jealousy, sexual promiscuity, and getting drunk during Communion. That's quite the church, isn't it? Can you imagine seeing those words on the church marquee? Yet, in the midst of unfinishedness, spiritual growth was taking place.

Just as God didn't recoil in horror at the Corinthians' unfinished state, He isn't afraid of your unfinishedness either. He was comfortable enough leaving a group of unfinished disciples. When Jesus died on the cross, the disciples were confused, afraid, and doubtful. They faced a future of finishing. Yet, in their state of incompletion, God used them to build a church that continues to revolutionize the world more than two thousand years later.

When I think of unfinishedness, I picture the wacky race I run every Thanksgiving Day called the Turkey Trot. (Actually, I don't run it; I jog it. Running indicates speed.) Anything goes in the Turkey Trot. Runners dress up in all kinds of crazy costumes. Over the 6.2-mile run, I'll encounter Santa pushing a beer keg, a woman dressed as Elvis, senior citizens running as reindeer (well, kind of—see jogging comment above), an old man with his pants so high it's gross, and just about anything you can imagine. It's so weird, but I love it! It's a great picture of the odd, weird, messy . . . and the journey. It's a scene similar to my life: odd, weird, occasionally gross, messy, but nonetheless a journey in which God is in the gradual process of sanctifying me. And as I move through life, I do so trusting that God isn't finished working in me, just like He isn't finished working in you.

Pursue God

God's Spirit and power ultimately change us. God molds our disorder into holiness. But within this process, we also have a free will. We can either choose to obey or reject God's ways. If we truly want to connect with God and be changed, then we must heed the words of Leviticus 20:7–8. They lay the groundwork for what is required of us: "Set yourselves apart for a holy life. Live a holy life, because I am GOD, your God. Do what I tell you; live the way I tell you. I am the GOD who makes you holy" (MSG, emphasis added).

I carefully chose the word *pursue* for this third action. I love this word because it communicates desire. Without desire, our actions are reduced to obligation rather than willful obedience. And a life of religious obligation yields spiritual apathy, performance-based religion, and a compartmentalized faith. But when we have genuine desire, we *want* to be close to God. We'll do anything to reach Him. Jesus responded to this type of desire—people interrupted Him, yelled out to Him, touched Him as He passed by, barged in on Him, and crashed through the ceiling to get to Him. In short, they *pursued* Him. Our own desire for Him can cause us to act in the very same ways. People *wanted* Jesus, and He did not disappoint them. He won't disappoint you either when He sees that your heart is filled with desire for Him. God cares much more about our desire to connect with Him than any sort of competence in connecting. The Pharisees were competent, but Jesus accused them of being actors (Matthew 23:5, 28). On the other hand, God can see right through incompetence to a heart that's tangled and untidy but longing for Him. He loves a heart—*any* heart—that is filled with desire.

He loves a heart—*any* heart—that is filled with desire.

When I first started dating my wife, Cathy, she asked me if I liked to dance. Without thinking I immediately shot back, "Yes!" Of course, I had no clue how to dance. The closest thing I had to a dance move was fielding a ground ball at a baseball game and falling. But that didn't matter. The amazing Cathy Guiso was asking me about dancing, and I responded out of desire. She could have asked me if I liked putting jalapeño juice in my eyes, and I would have said, "Absolutely! It's one of my favorite eyedrops." Because I desired to know this beautiful woman, I began to pursue things that didn't come naturally to me, and I began to pursue *her* . . . all the way to marriage. It's amazing what desire will do!

Talking to God, listening to Him, reading the Bible, and reflecting on His greatness may not come naturally, but pursue these things, because in so doing, you will be pursuing God. You are valuable to Him, and He wants to be intimate with you. *Pursue Him.*

The Specifics of Connecting

The paradox of this book is that while I'm trying to get you to embrace a simple formula—stop, be quiet, make a connection—connecting with God isn't really about a formula. It's about a relationship. So I want to make it clear that what I'm about to suggest isn't rigid. These are not actions on which you'll be evaluated or graded. Just figure out for yourself how to stop, be quiet, and connect with God, and then make it part of your everyday, ordinary, normal life. When you do, you will find yourself being spiritually refueled and feeling closer to God.

Personally, when I connect with God, I don't have one action I take each time. Of course, when I was a new Christian, I always tried to read at least one chapter of the Bible and pray for at least fifteen minutes a day. I thought this was *the only way* to refuel. Tragically, it brought a lot of guilt and feelings of failure when I didn't accomplish it. Today, though the foundation of my connections with God *usually* includes prayer and Scripture, I no longer feel the pressure to read a certain amount and pray through a list of prayer requests that I transcribe into my prayer journal. Now my connections with God are much more free-flowing. I read God's Word, but sometimes I do it at home, sometimes at work, and sometimes in my car. I keep a Bible in all three places. Other times I'll read verses I've written on three-by-five cards that I leave on my dashboard to meditate on while at stoplights. Or I reread my list of "favorite verses" that I've typed up and stored in my journal. Still other times I'll simply focus on God's Word by pondering verses that

I've committed to memory. I love God's Word and want to digest it as often as I can. I have no one way.

By the way, you don't always need to read the Bible in order to connect with God. Yet I find that people often feel guilty for not reading during their every connection with Him. Bible reading is definitely a great habit to develop, but remember, the printing press wasn't invented until the year 1440. That means that many of our brothers and sisters before us didn't even have a copy of God's Word. They couldn't have read it every day if they'd wanted to. But their lack of reading didn't make them lousy Christians.

I've found that the easiest way to get started in reading the Bible is to pick a book and read a short section (a chapter or less). Read it slowly. Try reading a few verses, and read them over several times. Don't read for speed; read for depth. Meditate or focus on one particular verse.

Don't read for speed; read for depth.

Maybe God's Word can come to you in a way you've never thought of before. There are a variety of great podcasts out there today on which people have simply read portions of Scripture, and you can download them to your iPod or computer. Many solid teachers also have their messages recorded and made easily available online. When you don't have time to read, you can certainly listen to the teaching of God's Word.

Finally, I encourage you, when you can, to find ways to hide God's Word in your heart. It will keep you from slipping. King David wrote, "I have hidden your word in my heart that I might not sin against you" (Psalm 119:11 NIV). It's so much easier to feel connected with God when you're not being harassed by a guilty conscience.

What about connecting with God through prayer? For me, prayer happens all throughout the day. It can happen anywhere—while merging into traffic, while putting on a shirt in the morning, while standing in line at a store, while struggling to write a sentence, or while walking to my car. The hows and wheres of connecting with God are limitless.

The beauty of prayer is that you can talk to God about whatever is on your mind. Pray for your friends, your family, your work situation, your kids at school. You may want to write out a prayer so you can be more deliberate. Or type one into a computer file and reread it often.

Another way to connect with God is just to think about Him. After you've stopped and become quiet, simply reflect on Him. *Who is God? What do I know about Him? God is good. God is loving. God is all-powerful. God made the universe . . .* Listen to the thoughts that come to you—all of them, not just the first one or two.

Here are a few more specific ideas that might help you connect with God:

» Write some of your favorite Bible verses on three-by-five cards and leave them in places where you'll be forced to stop occasionally (the car, your sock drawer, the kitchen table, near your toothbrush, etc.).

» Leave an extra Bible in the bathroom, on the back of the commode. Seriously. You read magazines there; why not the Word of God? Do you think God is embarrassed when you go to the bathroom? Uh, no . . . He created you.

» Establish spiritual habits that correspond to your daily routine. For example, when you get out of bed, pause for a second and thank God for another day to be alive. When you get in the shower, thank God for showering His grace and presence upon your life. When you get in the car, thank Him for your family. Try to develop several short connections that become part of the day-to-day routine of your life. Make up your own, but here are some to get you thinking:

Putting on your shoes: Thank God for directing your path (Psalm 23:3).

Stopping at a red light: Thank God for hearing your prayers (Matthew 7:7–11). He may answer them with a "yes" (green light), a "no" (red light), or a "wait" (yellow light).

Waiting in line: Think of how you don't have to wait to access the presence of God. Because of the Holy Spirit in your life, He is always with you (Acts 17:27–28).

Drinking water: Be reminded that Jesus promised water that would keep you from ever thirsting again (John 4:14).

Taking out the trash: Thank God for His willingness to offer you forgiveness and clean up your "trash" (1 John 1:9).

However you choose to connect with God, spiritual refueling will happen when you do. Within the small moments of each day, stop, be quiet, make a connection—set your mind and heart to focusing on God. When you connect daily, you access His love and His promises all over again. After all, it's in those promises—and the Person who gave them—that you put your faith. So make connections . . .

And see what happens.

///////////////////////////

This Week: After you make any type of connection with a friend (e-mail, text, phone, etc . . .), follow that with a short connection with God. Try it! See what happens.

Reflect: What do you think God might be saying to you after reading this chapter?

What aspect of connecting with God is the most difficult for you? How do you plan to stay refueled?

Prayer: Lord, thank You for allowing my faith to be messy and for Your grace in those times when I do, say, and think things that take me far from You. Thank You for redeeming my messiness and for giving me permission to hang an "Under Construction" sign

around my neck. Help me to faithfully pursue connections with You. Help me to see my life through
Your eyes and to know that You will continue to work
in me until the day I see You in heaven.

Designed for Greatness

B efore we close out this book, let's consider what might happen when you connect with God. After you learn to stop, be quiet, and make a connection, what is a realistic expectation?

I like to think about the result of connecting with God like this: when you were a little kid and someone asked what you wanted to be when you grew up, most likely you answered big—an astronaut, a firefighter, a teacher, a mommy, a doctor, a professional athlete, the president of the United States, an owner of a McDonald's Playland. Every kid is a dreamer. You never hear a kid say, "I want to grow up to be a drifter." Or, "I want to grow up to be very average." Or, "I'd like to become like my uncle Roofus, who drinks beer all day, never gets dressed, and watches TV until he passes out."

Can you remember when you wanted to be great at something? What did you dream about? I wanted to be a famous magician, one who knew how to pull a rabbit out of a hat and make a scarf disappear into thin air. I longed to make birds appear from nowhere and to saw people in half (especially the girl who lived next door, who tried to kiss me in second grade).

As I've gotten older, my desire for *doing* something great has decreased. Now, it's more about *being* great inwardly. I want to have a great character and let the actions of my life overflow from that depth. Nowadays I want to be a great friend, a great parent, and a great lover of life. I want to be skilled at showing compassion, celebrated for kindness, and adept at loving God and living for Him both at church *and* away from it. I don't want mediocrity to define me. I don't want my kids to think of their dad and say, "Ah, he was . . . okay." Or for Cathy to say, "As a spouse . . . he took up a lot of unnecessary space." Or for my friends to think, *Uh, actually Doug was really more of an acquaintance.* Or for God to say, "I never really knew him."

No one wakes up hoping for insecurity or chaos or misery. Everyone wants a great life, a life well lived.

The reason we don't want those other things is because God created us as original masterpieces designed for greatness. Your desires for greatness mean you want something more, something better, something richer and more meaningful for your life. That's a realistic expectation when you connect with God. You can expect your selfish desires to be replaced by genuine ones.

Perhaps when you hear the word *greatness*, you equate it with having your dream job and lots of money, vacations in the south of France, and an ice-cream maker within arm's reach of your bathtub. Okay, but I'd love to point you in the direction of actually *developing* greatness—something that's measured by your life and character rather than your status, stuff, and savings. What is it that you really want? Start narrowing the options by identifying what you *don't* want.

You don't want your friendships to be average.

You don't want your marriage to be routine.

You don't want your career to be purposeless and passionless.

You don't want your bad habits or addictions to define you.

You don't want your kids to not really know you.

You don't want material things to fill emotional and spiritual voids.

You don't want to be consumed by conflicts.

You don't want to spend all your free time in front of the TV or computer.

You don't want to live a forgettable life.

The great life you want is something much more significant than being able to make a bird appear from a magic hat (although that is awesome . . . as is the ice-cream maker by the tub). A great life requires more than a big house, a new car, or a promotion. And you know that there has to be a better route toward greatness than a TV show, a self-help book, or a bottle of top-shelf tequila.

Fortunately, Jesus presented a "how to" to help our "want to." You and I want our lives to be marked by greatness, and Jesus gave us a road map to get there. But I have to warn you: the "how to" Jesus described is not a comfortable route!

Anatomy of a Life Well Lived

To give us an idea of what Jesus' route to greatness looks like, I want to look at some people who lived such significant lives that we're still talking about them two thousand years after they died. The people I'm referring to are Jesus' earliest followers, commonly known as His disciples. We can learn a lot about a life well lived from them.

> There has to be a better route toward greatness than a TV show, a self-help book, or a bottle of top-shelf tequila.

I've been suggesting in this book that to succeed at connecting with God, you don't need to compare yourself to the super-Christians. The funny thing about Jesus' disciples is that none of them would have fit in that category. I've always found satisfaction in the fact that the guys closest to Jesus seemed like very ordinary people—even knuckleheads at times. They were simply fishermen and business owners and regular folks. Yet they were part of God's universe-changing plan.

How are you and I like them today?

They Were Followers of Jesus

The early disciples followed Jesus. It sounds like such a simple idea—following Jesus. It's not simple, but it does form the foundation for greatness.

At first glance you might think that it wasn't too

hard for the early disciples to follow Jesus—all they needed to do was set down their fishing nets. How hard could that have been? Say good-bye to smelling like mackerel and getting fish hooks stuck in your fingers? What a hardship . . .

Jesus invited them to a life of *sacrifice*. And today the invitation to be a follower of Jesus still requires sacrifice. The disciples had to put down their nets—and their livelihoods—to follow Him.

What do you need to put down in order to follow Jesus? What might you need to sacrifice in order to stop, be quiet, and make a connection?

They Learned Along the Way

None of the disciples knew much when they first followed Jesus. They had a lot of questions. They frequently made mistakes or misunderstood what Jesus was trying to teach. But that didn't hold them back.

I imagine a scenario like this: A crowd is around Jesus, and a particular woman can't get close enough to Him to ask a question, so she asks one of His followers. Let's pretend it's Peter. She says, "Umm, excuse me, but did He really say that we are to love our enemies?"

Another guy walks up and asks, "Uh, about that whole turning-the-other-cheek thing . . . He's not serious, is He?"

The early disciples learned the ropes of following Jesus by jumping in with both feet. The more they walked with Jesus, the more they learned about His ways and the better able they became to embrace His ways and articulate His revolutionary teaching to others.

What are you doing to learn more about Jesus and His ways?

They Experienced Exciting Times

A lot of unexpected things can happen to you when you follow Jesus. They certainly happened to the early disciples. Can you picture the excitement at the beginning of their journey with Jesus? "Uh, sorry, Jesus can't see you right now. He's busy raising Lazarus from the dead. Then He has plans to cast demons out of a madman and into pigs. Soon after, He'll be taking our leftover food and feeding an army. Never a dull moment with Jesus."

Same reality today. Sometimes the exciting times come when we're put in situations we never would have dreamed of. Maybe it's when we step out in faith and serve. Or when we pursue an opportunity to show compassion to the hurting. There can be amazing excitement connected to a life that is committed to following Jesus.

How are you experiencing excitement in your life because you follow Jesus?

They Experienced Difficult Times

Life is seldom easy for anyone. If you were an early disciple of Jesus, you encountered storms and angry crowds and a government that often wanted to see you dead. Following Jesus was the pathway to a life of greatness, but rarely was it an easy or pain-free path.

Following Jesus was the pathway to a life of greatness, but rarely was it an easy or pain-free path.

The same is true for us today. If you're a modern disciple, you encounter a world of temptations that didn't exist in days gone by, or the inner struggle with materialism and greed; or maybe you have to make unpopular decisions at work or in your community.

Perhaps the difficulty is trying to love someone who is hard to love. Or it could be an outer struggle, where your hardships, tragedies, medical conditions, or financial crises are obvious. Maybe you encounter intense spiritual opposition like never before. Before you followed Jesus, it was a lot easier just to sit around on weekends and enjoy a ball game. But now there's a call to follow Jesus and serve, not just on weekends, but daily.

God uses these difficult times to transform us into the likeness of His Son. Plus, the truly worthwhile things in life often wouldn't be worthwhile if they came too easily.

What difficulties in your life might God be using to change you?

They Obeyed His Instructions

The early disciples were called to be participants, not merely observers, in God's plan. Jesus knew that a life well lived was a life that involved service, not sitting around watching reruns of *Oprah*. A life well lived includes helping others. Jesus told His disciples: "Go to the lost . . . Tell them that the kingdom is here. Bring health to the sick . . . Touch the untouchables . . . You have been treated generously, so live generously" (Matthew 10:6–8 MSG).

That's our call as well. Jesus invites us to a life of obedience and service. Those aren't words that translate well in this day and age. Why? Because obedience is often at odds with convenience. But obedience leads to the full life. Jesus even went so far as to say that our love for Him is seen through obedience.

Where are you personally sacrificing convenience for obedience?

They Were Rewarded

The call to follow Jesus can seem overwhelming at times. And we pastor-types have done a great job at taking the simple words of Jesus ("Follow Me") and making them complex. But Jesus told His disciples, "If you give even a cup of cold water to one of the least of my followers, you will surely be rewarded" (Matthew 10:42). That doesn't sound too hard, does it? Just giving a cup of cold water to someone who looks thirsty—or whatever small act of service you're called to do?

There's a promise in that verse as well. A life of following Jesus and obeying His ways is an adventure full of challenges, surprises, and—hang on to your pancreas—*rewards*. God's rewards may be revealed on earth, but we'll also have other rewards waiting in heaven for all eternity.

Where do you see God rewarding your obedience?

You and I might not have had the opportunity to walk on the same ground as Jesus, but we can still experience some of the same results of the first disciples by walking Jesus' way. We simply must be more intentional about connecting with God. Jesus' disciples were connected at the hip. Day and night for a few years, they ate, camped, walked, and shared everything together. To share in the fullness that God has planned for us requires some key decisions.

Where to Start, Right Now, Today

Make a decision to follow Jesus. A decision to leap over guilt. A decision to put down comparison. A decision to live a noncompartmentalized, integrated faith. A decision to be refueled. The decision to:

Stop.

Be quiet.

Make a connection.

Your invitation is to decide to connect with God and refuel your soul. That's an action only you can take.

Just so you're really sure about what happens when you make this decision, let me reiterate what you're doing when you refuel your soul. Really, refueling means two things:

1. You're Filling Yourself Up with God

God is the ultimate power source. He's all the gasoline and hydroelectricity and nuclear power and wind-generated energy you could ever want or need. When you connect yourself directly to the Source of all power, your spiritual tank will be full, and you will have what you need for each day. That's what it means to be a spiritual self-feeder. Going to church each Sunday hoping to be refueled by someone else will never provide you with all you need. You need to learn to connect with God on your own to keep your spiritual tank filled.

It's such a simple truth: everything needs a power source. Cars work best with gas in their tanks. A toaster works only when it's plugged in. It doesn't matter how pretty the toaster is, or how much the toaster cost, or if the toaster grew up in the church kitchen. If it's not plugged in, it doesn't get power. And you don't get toast—you're stuck with bread.

Jesus spelled out this connection theory very clearly when He said, "I am the vine; you are the branches. Those who *remain* in me, and I in them, will produce much fruit. For *apart from me* you can do nothing" (John 15:5, emphasis added). The goal is to stay connected to the One who gives life.

2. You're Living a Life That's Designed for Greatness

When you continually refuel your soul, there's a purpose to it. Your life is designed to glorify God. And when you glorify God, you live an amazing life no matter what happens in and around you.

God's fuel works in connection to faith. Each day when you stop, become quiet, and connect with God, you are actively doing your part in the refueling process, taking action before you ever experience His power. Action in anticipation is *faith*. You take action (stop, be quiet, make a connection) and anticipate (trust) that God will act. And He will be true to His word. God will change lives. He will love and care for and lead you in how you should live. Hebrews 11:1 gives us a good picture of this. It defines faith as the confident assurance that what we hope for is going to happen.

///

Action in anticipation is faith.

///

Did you catch the sequence here? God's invitation to live an amazing life is always with us. His promises have been given to us in His Word. So believing His promises, we act first, and then God responds to our faith.

Are you like me and would prefer God's power to be evident before you display faith? Oh yeah! I want power *before* I do the right thing, *before* I resolve a crisis, and *way before* I do anything risky for the Lord. But the Bible clearly reveals that God supplies power along the way *according to* our faith. It's like when Peter walked on the water (Matthew 14:22–32). Jesus was already standing in the wind and waves, and He invited Peter to step out of the boat and come to Him. "Take courage," Jesus said to him. "Don't be afraid."

So Peter stepped over the side. He had to act first, and then Christ's power kicked in for him. Sure, he eventually sank, but don't forget that he was the only one willing to get out of the boat. Peter acted on what he knew. He believed Jesus and stepped forward in faith. It was only then that God empowered him. The good news is, the same God who has empowered His people like Peter throughout the ages can infuse your life with power too.

What might faith look like in your life today? Let's consider a few scenarios:

If you're investigating Jesus and genuinely seeking God, then step out. Start walking in the direction of Jesus. Go to church. Start reading a Bible. Ask questions. Begin talking to God. Join a small group to connect with others on their spiritual journeys. Take steps of faith in the direction of committing your life to Christ, and watch what God does along the way.

If you're already a Christ-follower, perhaps you need to reconcile with a family member or resolve a broken friendship. Take those steps in faith. Call that person and ask for forgiveness. Not because you want to or because it's easy, but because you're stepping out in faith, being obedient to do the right thing, and trusting God's power to show up.

Perhaps you're living with someone and not married. You want God's blessing on your relationship, don't you? Then one of you needs to pack a suitcase and move out until you make your relationship legal in the eyes of God. Have faith that God will give you the power to develop a relationship according to His standards.

Are these difficult steps to take? Absolutely! But are they essential for your life? Extremely! When you do take action, you can trust that God will give you power as power is needed.

No Longer Empty

My friend, your spiritual tank does not need to be empty again. Your soul longs for the fullness of life that God promises. When you regularly connect with God, you not only access the power and guidance you need for each day, but you also invest in eternity—where your real home is going to be. When you take time to refuel your soul, you're doing something that will last forever.

Life is so much better when your spiritual tank is full. But if you are nearing empty, please know there is hope. Anyone can follow the simplicity I've laid out in this book. Let me repeat it one last time:

Stop.

Be quiet.

Make a connection.

That's all there is to it. The plan is sustainable. It's powerful, and it works. God promises to show His people how to truly live. So when we regularly connect with God, we can count on it. Not only that, but our souls are restocked. Emptiness diminishes. We have a new power and spiritual energy for each day. Then welcome to your new life! One that's continually being *refueled*.

///////////////////////////

This week . . . and beyond: Continue to find stopping points in your life and quiet moments to focus on connecting with God. Pray that God will reveal even more ways to connect with Him. Share what you've learned (and possibly this book) with a friend.

Reflect: What do you think God might be saying to you after reading this chapter?

What would a life of "greatness" look like for you?

Prayer: Lord, thank You for Your grace, mercy, and love, and that You refuse to give up on me. Thank

You that You continue to pursue a relationship with me, and that You sent your Son to provide a way for me to connect with You. I know that when You ask me to do something, You will always provide the ways and the means to do it. And I know that when I ask, You'll give me the discipline, the desire, and the power to connect with You throughout the day, every day. Please continue to transform my heart as I continue to pursue You faithfully.

//

Discussion Questions: How to Get the Most from This Book

There are at least three ways to use this book... four, if you consider using it as a doorstop, which I don't actually recommend.

You can:

» Read it alone and journal through it using the discussion questions on the following pages.

» Read it and discuss it with a spouse or friend.

» Read a chapter a week with your small group, and pick one or two of the suggested questions to get you talking.

Reading this book through in one sitting is certainly possible. You can probably finish most of it while waiting in line at the DMV. But my prayer is that you'll reflect on the material one chapter at a time, either in a group or by yourself.

I tried to write some questions that would stimulate thought and discussion. The questions are designed to help you dig beneath the surface, to get to the real issues that have been keeping you from consistently connecting with God in a way that keeps your spiritual tank full. They'll also help you identify practical ways to apply what you've learned and to develop habits to keep you from running on empty.

Obviously, the care and feeding of your spiritual life is your responsibility, and you've taken a great first step by choosing to read *Refuel*, so take full advantage of this study guide.

If you are reading this book with others: All groups are different, so choose questions that suit your group, ones you believe will inspire good discussion. And don't feel pressure to answer all of the discussion questions. Your goal shouldn't be to check off "answered all questions" from an imaginary list, but to discover and adopt practical ways to connect with God.

To help you get the most from your small group time, you can view three videos at www. saddlebackresources.com. These videos are short, introductory teaching sessions that give my heart and a different perspective on the chapters you have read. My prayer is that they will help your group time as well as encourage each member to stay refueled with God.

If you are reading through on your own: Build in some time to reflect on the questions, and make sure to use the blank spaces as you would a personal journal. Have your favorite reading Bible handy to dig a little deeper into the passages used in each chapter. Interact with the material. Make the book your own.

As with any study guide or system, it needs to work for you.

Chapter 1—I'm a Spiritual Loser

Discussing with others: consider returning to page 16 and sharing your answers to the reflection questions before jumping into the following questions.

» How have you experienced spiritual emptiness in your own life?

» I listed some of my personal signs of emptiness on page 4. Which of these signs appear on your personal list? What are other indicators that reveal when your spiritual life is nearing the red zone?

» Which of these signs have you tried to hide from others? Why do you think you need to hide your spiritual emptiness?

» Who is one person you can trust with the truth of your emptiness?

» What are some of your current (or past) challenges to having a good "quiet time"?

» When have you compared your spiritual life to that of another person? Who and why? Would you be willing to admit that you're following somebody's unrealistic spiritual example?

Chapter 2—Ditch the Guilt

//

Discussing with others: consider returning to page 34 and sharing your answers to the reflection questions before jumping into the following questions.

» How does guilt show up in your life?

» How can you know the difference between guilt as a motivation from God and the false guilt you heap on yourself? Why might that be important to know?

» What "heavy load" are you carrying today? (See page 20.) Why do you think you are carrying it?

» What is an example of a time you have experienced a "compartmentalized faith" (pages 21–25)?

» Many believe that "living for God means not blowing it in the big areas of life." How do you decide what is "big" and what is "not so big"? Why is obedience in the "smaller" areas of life often so difficult?

» What are some things that never seem to fall off of your personal to-do list? What are some things that you wish weren't on that list? Why?

» In this chapter I listed three reasons why we need to be continually refilled spiritually:

> *Being Busy Doesn't Satisfy*
> *Our Souls Long to Be Filled*
> *There's Something More Ahead*

Which of these Biblical truths can you most indentify with? Why?

» What do you think the apostle Paul meant when he wrote: "We . . . know that as long as we are home in the body, we are away from the Lord" (2 Cor. 5:6)? What does that tell you about Paul's focus and values? What does it tell you about the need to regularly connect with God? How would you rephrase that statement in your own terms?

Chapter 3—Stop

Discussing with others: consider returning to page 54 and sharing your answers to the reflection questions before jumping into the following questions.

» Think of a time when you were experiencing something new, such as starting an exercise program or learning a foreign language. What did it feel like to be a beginner?

» What are some signs that people close to you may be worn out, drained, exhausted, and fatigued? What are your personal signs?

» As our days fill up with activity, our time is used up and we don't get it back. What has filled up your life in the past? What would you like it to be filled with?

» How much margin do you have in your life? What steps can you take to create more margin? Who is someone you can ask to hold you accountable?

» In this chapter I wrote about four lies that can take root in our lives:

> *There's just not enough time to do everything.*
> *I'm just in a busy season right now.*
> *But this is really, really important.*
> *Success and busyness are synonyms.*

Which of these lies do you most often return to? What would help you to stop believing this lie?

» What does our culture say about "stopping"? How does that cultural pressure to fill our days affect the people you know? How does it affect you?

» Who is someone you know who treats busyness as a badge of honor? How does it affect the way they live their life? What is attractive to you about busyness? Is that attraction healthy or unhealthy?

» Think about when you've had to say no to your boss, your coworkers, your friends, and your family members. When was it easy and when was it difficult? Why?

» On page 48–49, I offer some practical pauses, or "stopping points." Take a few minutes to think of others that could apply directly to your life. List them.

Chapter 4—Be Quiet

///

Discussing with others: consider returning to page 74 and sharing your answers to the reflection questions before jumping into the following questions.

» What is your favorite form of distracting noise? (See pages 58–60.) Why?

» Does your mind wander when you attempt to be quiet? Where do your thoughts usually go? Work . . . family . . . fears . . . the future?

» Have your experiences with quiet and/or silence made you want it more often or less often? Why?

» I mentioned three "enemies of silence" on pages 58–61:

> The Noise of Worry
> The Noise of Wanting
> The Noise of Procrastinating

Which of these three do you come up against
most often? Why do you think it's difficult for
you to block this noise out?

» Do you feel like you have ever heard God's
voice? What was the situation? What did He say?

» What noises are drowning out God's
"personalized whisper" to you?

» What are some baby steps that you might be
able to take that would lead to a quieter life?

Chapter 5—Make a Connection

Discussing with others: consider returning to page 93 and sharing your answers to the reflection questions before jumping into the following questions.

» What are some of the different ways you stay connected with your friends and family members? Could any of those methods be used to make connections with God? If so, how?

» Do you believe that God really wants to connect with His people? Do you really believe He wants to connect with you? What do you base your belief on?

» How could this basic truth (that God wants to connect with you) change the way you approach Him?

» If you truly desire to connect with God, why is it often so difficult?

» What is the difference between obligation and obedience when it comes to time with God?

» What are some potential outcomes of coming to God out of obligation? How about out of obedience?

» I wrote that God wants to turn our "messiness into holiness." How does that make you feel? Have you seen it happen in your life? Share one example.

» What are some specific ways you will connect with God this week?

Chapter 6—Designed for Greatness

///

Discussing with others: consider returning to page 111 and sharing your answers to the reflection questions before jumping into the following questions.

» What is the first thing that comes to your mind when you hear the word "greatness?" How about the word "significance"?

» How does it make you feel to read that none of Jesus' disciples were "super Christians"? Why might that truth provide hope? Why is that type of hope important?

» How are you currently experiencing excitement in your life simply because you are following Jesus?

» What current difficulties in your life might God be using to change you?

» Can you think of any place you are currently sacrificing convenience for obedience? Is it easy, tough, rewarding, etc.? How do "acts of obedience" make you feel?

» *Stop*
  Be Quiet
  Make a Connection

  Which of these three steps needs the most immediate attention in order for you to begin building a habit of a refueled connection with God? Write it down, share it with a friend or your small group. Ask for accountability, and go after it.

» After finishing this book, what is one take-away that you will try to apply?

» Who is one person in your life whom you could now take with you on the journey of learning to refuel? Consider helping a friend, child, coworker, spouse, or neighbor discover the joy of being refueled on a daily basis.

Share your refueling story with me at
doug@dougfields.com.

About the Author

With thirty years of experience in ministry, Doug Fields is currently a teaching pastor at Saddleback Community Church in Mission Viejo, California, where he has been on staff since 1992. In addition to his teaching responsibilities, he also oversees all the life-stage groups (children, youth, college, etc.) at the more than twenty thousand-member church.

Doug has authored or coauthored more than fifty books (see www.dougfields.com). His highly acclaimed *Purpose Driven Youth Ministry* has helped shape the course of youth ministry worldwide. Other best-selling books he has authored include *The One Minute Bible, Your First*

Two Years in Youth Ministry, and Congratulations . . . You're Gifted!

Doug and his wife, Cathy, have three teenage children.